MISSING IN MEXICO

A True Mystery

Robert Richard Downes

Longhornbar Books LLC

Copyright © 2022 Longhornbar Books LLC

All rights reserved

The characters and events portrayed in this book are fictitious. Any similarity to real persons, living or dead, is coincidental and not intended by the author.

No part of this book may be reproduced, or stored in a retrieval system, or transmitted in any form or by any means, electronic, mechanical, photocopying, recording, or otherwise, without express written permission of the publisher.

ISBN-13: 979-8-9874217-0-3

Cover design by: Laura Downes
Printed in the United States of America

I want to dedicate this work to the memory of Barbara Charline Jordan. She was a lawyer, educator, politician, and leader in the civil rights movement. She was the first African American elected to the Texas Senate after Reconstruction and as a representative to the United States House of Representatives was a vocal participant in the Watergate hearings. She was also a friend and my professor at the Lyndon B. Johnson School of Public Affairs in Austin, Texas where she taught me the importance of justice and the rule of law.

CONTENTS

Title Page
Copyright
Foreword   1
Wednesday, June 9, 1982 - The Search Begins   3
The Missing Professor   12
Wednesday, June 16 - The Search Continues   17
Monday, June 28 - The Truck   25
Tuesday, June 29 – the Search for the Body   32
Wednesday, June 30 - Georgia Sheriffs   39
Friday, July 2 - A Body Found?   48
Saturday, July 3 - A Search for the Search   53
Sunday, July 4 - Election Day   59
Tuesday, July 6 - The Rains Begin   66
Friday, July 9 - The Reward   69
Sunday, July 11 - The Body Found?   75
Tuesday, July 13 - The Body Identified?   81
Wednesday, July 14 - Delays and Doubts   88

Thursday, July 15 - A Body Shipped	91
Friday, July 16 - Doubts Confirmed	95
Sunday, July 18 — The Consul General Visits Culiacán	103
Friday, July 23 – The Other Shoe Drops	114
Monday, July 26 - The Suspects Are Indicted	117
Rising Congressional Concern	121
Sunday, August 1 - The Search Continues	126
Sunday, August 22 to Monday, August 23 - Allegations of Torture	136
Tuesday, August 24 — The Body Found?	138
September	143
October to December	157
January and February 1983	173
March through July -- The Manzanillo Sighting	179
July – The Prosecution Acts	192
July - Congress Reacts	197
July – The Judge Decides	205
August through December	210
1984	218
Saturday, April 20, 1985 – A Body Found	224
Tuesday, April 23 – A Body Identified	228
Wednesday, April 24 to Tuesday, May 21 - A Thorough Examination	234

Wednesday, May 22 through December	243
1986	250
The Reward	259
The Final Developments	264
Afterword	266
Acknowledgements	270
About The Author	271

FOREWORD

This is the story of the 1982 disappearance of Nicholas Wickham Schrock on the highways of western Mexico. Schrock was an American professor traveling from Arizona to teach for the summer in Guadalajara, Mexico. His disappearance had a profound impact on my professional career and my outlook on life. His story demonstrates the lengths that U.S. consular officers abroad go to assist Americans in distress and the limitations of those efforts. As such, it is largely written from the perspective of the consular officers searching for Professor Schrock. Finally, after working on his disappearance over an intense period and learning quite a bit about his life, I wanted to ensure that such a once-vibrant person would not be forgotten.

I do not intend to dwell on the macabre aspects of the case and wish to respect the memory of Professor Schrock at all times. A substantial portion of the information imparted here comes from my memory of the actual events, supplemented by substantial resources received from the U.S. Department of State through Freedom of Information Act (FOIA) requests. This was particularly helpful in covering events that occurred after my departure from the U.S. Consulate in Mazatlán, Mexico in mid-1983, although I kept in touch with those serving in Mazatlán after I left. As the story follows events from literally forty years ago and comes partially from memories, there may be minor discrepancies, but I have done my best to cross-check as many facts as possible.

While I have mentioned some names in the book, largely U.S. and Mexican officials, I deliberately left out the names of most individuals to protect their privacy even if they were mentioned by name in the FOIA materials. There are some exceptions, such as officials at the University of Colorado in Boulder and American Graduate School of International Management, Thunderbird Campus (hereinafter Thunderbird) in Arizona who worked actively to locate Professor Schrock. I have also carefully avoided disclosing any possible classified matters and although some of my source materials referred to as "cables" were originally classified as confidential, these have since been declassified. (I am using "cables" as a shorthand term for diplomatic and consular telegrams transmitted internally between overseas consulates and embassies and the Department of State in Washington, D.C.) Even with these few cables, I have avoided matters that after forty years might be deemed overly sensitive. The draft text was submitted to the Department of State for review before publication.

I have no intention of profiting from the telling of the tale and intend to donate the net proceeds of any money received from the book sales to charity in Professor Schrock's name.

WEDNESDAY, JUNE 9, 1982
- THE SEARCH BEGINS

I first heard the name Nicholas Wickham Schrock on June 9, 1982. Little did I know at the time that the search for Professor Schrock would have a major influence on my professional work for the next year in Mexico and, in some ways, a profound influence on my diplomatic career and on my outlook on life. It was a quiet Wednesday afternoon and I was sitting in my office on the second floor of an old Spanish-style residence that the U.S. government had leased to house the American Consulate in Mazatlán, Mexico. It was in the old part of the city and only a few blocks from the port and was a bit rundown. While once perhaps elegant, the old residence was now shabby. It was not the sort of building one expects to house a U.S. government facility, but it was comfortable, well-located and inexpensive.

We were normally closed to the public at that time of day, except for emergency services to U.S. citizens, to allow us a quiet time to take care of the myriad of paperwork challenges that were part of the daily life of a consular officer. I was reviewing cable traffic (incoming diplomatic messages) from Washington, the Embassy in Mexico City and other consulates. As we only had an aging Western Union teletypewriter for communications – archaic for diplomatic operations even at that time – all of the message traffic was unclassified. The fact that we relied on a Western

Union machine, as opposed to a dedicated State Department system, aided in our work, including in the search for Professor Schrock, as we could receive information and communications quickly and directly from outside sources. This functioned as a sort of early email system. It also meant that it broke down frequently, so at times we were limited to the telephone as our only means of communication. This was well before the advent of cellphones, so we relied heavily on landlines. As Mazatlán was a small consular operation, we seldom dealt with classified material. Most consular communications, while subject to privacy protections, were routine matters.

As I mentioned, I was reviewing cable traffic. Even after more than forty years, I remember that the coffee in the mug on my desk had long become cold and I was thinking of starting a fresh pot of coffee when suddenly one message caught my immediate attention. This was a welfare-and-whereabouts request from Consulate General Guadalajara regarding a visiting professor traveling to that city to take part in a summer teaching program. The Consulate Mazatlán received many welfare-and-whereabouts messages regarding missing U.S. citizens from the State Department in Washington's operations center, but most were pretty vague. For example: "The mother of John Doe called the Department to help locate her son. She thinks he is either in Mexico or Colombia. He has brown hair and is about 5'10" in height. Please look for him."

There is little we can do in most cases other than to check to see if the individual was registered in the Consular District, a voluntary process that many of our long-term U.S. residents and "snowbirds" participated in, or to contact the usual sources – police, hospitals, morgues and funeral homes – to see if they had any U.S. citizens matching that description. One of the things the Consulate did, as did other overseas U.S. consular operations, was to develop a substantial web of contacts throughout the two Mexican states – Sinaloa and Nayarit – that made up our consular district. We worked persistently to encourage those contacts to notify us if a U.S. citizen was injured, arrested or died or otherwise needed our assistance. In general, it worked well. I would often be called at home in the middle of the night by a contact to let me know an American had been injured or killed and at what hospital or morgue he was. The former was particularly important as we would immediately go to the hospital to ensure the American was getting needed care, agreeing to fund it. if necessary. The police generally called us the next day to report an arrest and we would then, on a priority basis, go visit the incarcerated.

The striking difference regarding Guadalajara's report on the professor's disappearance and the majority of our other welfare and whereabouts messages was in its detail. While it was extremely brief, it implied that immediate action was necessary. The message read:

Subject: W/W: Nicholas Schrock

1. Post has been informed by subject's colleagues at the Autonomous University of Guadalajara that he is six days overdue. Mr. Schrock left Phoenix on May 30 for Guadalajara via Hermosillo, Culiacán, and Mazatlán. He is participating in a program of visiting professors from the American Graduate School of International Management. To date, his wife in Phoenix has also not heard from him.

2. Schrock is 43-year-old, white male, 135 pounds, 5'8", medium brown hair, glasses. He is driving a 1980 Datsun Super cab pickup truck, cream-colored, with Colorado plates.
    3. Please advise of efforts.

We later learned that the Consulate General in Guadalajara had received a telegram from Thunderbird School officials on June 7 stating the professor, scheduled to arrive on June 2, was overdue. While the June 9 message I was reviewing was addressed to Washington, D.C. for action with only an information copy to Mazatlán, we knew from reading it that we needed to take immediate action instead of waiting for instructions. While it was always possible that the professor had taken a side trip or been delayed by problems with his truck, the fact that he had not communicated with his wife or colleagues for almost a week after his expected arrival made this unlikely, even based on the limited information we had at the time.

To provide some additional background, Mazatlán was one of the smallest of the seven U.S. Consulates spread out across Mexico that served as branches of the U.S. Embassy in Mexico City. The city itself is the largest port between San Diego and Panama and, as a result, the United States has had a Consulate there off-and-on since 1835. Due to its pleasant climate and long beaches, it was a popular destination for tourists from the United States and Canada, with many arriving on cruise ships. Almost all of the work at the Consulate focused on consular matters such as issuing nonimmigrant visas, accepting passports applications and assisting U.S. citizens involved in theft, death and injury cases.

I was one of two Vice Consuls serving at the post under the direction of the Principal Officer, Consul John St. Denis, an experienced mid-level officer that had transferred from the Diplomatic Security part of the State Department to Consular work. Newly married, I was beginning my second year with the State Department and had been in Mazatlán less than six months. The other Vice Consul, Michael Oreste, was also new to the Foreign Service and had arrived at post only a month or two before me. We had, in addition, a very efficient staff of five Mexican nationals that were an integral and important part of our operations.

Despite the activities of the Sinaloa drug cartel and other such groups in the area, our Consular District was not considered particularly dangerous for U.S. citizens at the time. Yes, we had deaths – I handled the deaths of five unrelated U.S. citizens during my first week of working in Mazatlán in December 1981and the great majority were either of elderly tourists with pre-existing health issues or automobile accidents. The stretch of the InterAmerican Highway that ran through Sinaloa and Nayarit was particularly dangerous due to its poor condition and heavy truck traffic. The secondary highways and roads were even worse. Unlit broken-down vehicles and free-ranging cattle were a real danger at night. The Embassy forbade its Consular Officers in rural areas from driving outside the cities at night due to the traffic danger. Because of this, we were especially sensitive to reports of Americans that might have been injured while driving across our district.

After conferring with the Principal Officer and the other Vice Consul, we and our staff began to make calls to the local police in Mazatlán, as well as to hospitals, transit authorities and the Green Angels, a group that assisted motorists in distress along major highways and roads. We had a long list of such organizations that we relied on in such cases. We extended our search efforts to Culiacán (the capital of the state of Sinaloa) and to Los Mochis in the north as well as to Tepic, Nayarit in the south as these would have been on the route of someone driving from Arizona to Guadalajara. These efforts continued through the next day and on the morning of June 10 without anyone reporting sighting Professor Schrock. We also called hotels, although this process took much longer given that Mazatlán and other parts of Sinaloa were popular tourist attractions and had many hotels. We sent in a routine cable the next morning reporting our activities in this case. Being a small Consulate in a remote part of Mexico, our normal operations were quite busy with us often working late and on weekends to keep up with the workload. However, since this was a case of a possibly injured or endangered U.S. citizen, we gave it a higher priority.

The initial message from Guadalajara was also sent to our Consulate in Hermosillo, Sonora, which would also have been on the route driven by Professor Schrock. On June 16, Hermosillo reported that Mexican immigration authorities had confirmed Professor Schrock's May 30 entry into Mexico at Nogales but provided little additional information. The message noted that the Hermosillo Consulate's staff had checked with funeral homes, hospitals, police (including the Mexican Federal Highway Police) in Hermosillo and the other major cities in Sonora. No one besides the immigration authorities reported having any contact with Schrock. Consulate General Guadalajara subsequently reported similar efforts and results.

An inevitable result of making a widespread broadcast for an U.S. citizen in trouble is that you begin to receive a large number of reports of sightings or other noise that each needs to be carefully checked or verified. Most often these reports prove erroneous. This was certainly true almost immediately in the case of Schrock but continued throughout the months of search for him. On June 10, for example, our staff in Mazatlán received:

> a report by telephone call from the police in Nayarit of the death of an unidentified American. The only description provided was that the subject appeared to be in his late thirties, with long brown hair. He appeared to be dead anywhere from several days to several weeks. The police assumed he was American because he "looked American." The body was without documentation and personal effects ...

On further inquiries regarding height, age and other physical characteristics, it appeared that even if the deceased turned out to be a U.S. citizen, it was unlikely to be Professor Schrock. We also noted in our report that we planned to send Vice Consul Oreste to Tepic in the southern part of our Consular district on June 21 to try to determine if the body was that of a U.S. citizen. Tepic is a several hour drive from Mazatlán which would necessitate an overnight stay and fully occupy one of our officers for two days, including visiting Americans imprisoned in that city and other consular matters. To further complicate our staffing issues, shortly after our receipt of the initial June 9 welfare and whereabouts cable regarding Professor Schrock, our Consul, St. Denis, was subject to a routine transfer and so we were down an experienced officer. To assist us until a new Principal Officer arrived, the Consulate General in Monterrey loaned us an experienced second-tour officer, Ron Kramer, to serve as acting Principal Officer in Mazatlán and to help us in the interim and to oversee our operations. He proved a sound choice as he was a diligent officer and instantly became an integral part of the team.

Our efforts to find Professor Schrock also elicited a report on June 14 from police officials of a U.S. citizen arrested in Los Mochis in the northern part of our Consular district and on the route that Schrock would have driven. After a number of telephone exchanges with the police on that date, we determined, based on their description of the individual and his identity documents, that the young man arrested was probably not Professor Schrock and also probably not a U.S citizen. This is but one of the many leads we had to respond to and carefully check out in the initial days of the search.

While the Consulate staffs of Guadalajara, Hermosillo and Mazatlán were actively searching for Professor Schrock and chasing down numerous reports and leads, there were also developments at the Embassy in Mexico City. The U.S. Ambassador to Mexico at the time was actor John Gavin, President Ronald Reagan's good friend. Ambassador Gavin often paraphrased Victor Mature, saying, "I am not an actor, and I have two dozen movies to prove it." He had appeared as Julius Caesar in Stanley Kubrick's "Spartacus" and as well in Alfred Hitchcock's "Psycho." He had a commanding presence, being 6 feet, 4 inches tall and was fluent in Spanish.

You noticed him when he entered the room. While he may not have known the details of U.S.-Mexican relations, when he was in Washington, he could have a private lunch with the President of the United States. As a result, he was extremely popular with the Mexican government and public as the President was showing his respect for Mexico by sending his close friend as Ambassador. He arrived in Mexico in June of 1981 and served as Ambassador for five years until June of 1986.

On June 15 Ambassador Gavin received a phone call from a professor at Thunderbird who had been his classmate at Stanford. While the Ambassador later told us privately that the individual calling him was not a close friend, he did remember him from his days at the University and so was definitely interested in taking the call. The Ambassador's old Stanford alumni asked the Ambassador to take a personal interest in the case of his missing colleague. Ambassador Gavin agreed to do so and shortly thereafter set up a task force in the Embassy to monitor progress of the case to ensure the Consulates had sufficient resources for their search efforts and to provide him frequent briefings. While the task force marginally increased our workload in terms of generating new requests for information from the Embassy, we did receive additional support and resources that were helpful in the coming days.

THE MISSING PROFESSOR

Nicholas Wickham Schrock was born January 17, 1939, in Perry, Ohio. He stood 5 feet, 9 inches tall, weighed about 140 pounds with brown hair and hazel eyes and he wore glasses. He was an avid jogger and had no history of serious medical issues, although he did wear shoe inserts to support his arches.

According to his wife, Ruth Schrock, he was a professor of economics on a one-year sabbatical leave from the University of Colorado, where he had taught since 1969. He received his bachelor's degree in economics from Case Institute of Technology (now Case Western Reserve University) in 1961, a master's degree from San Diego State University in 1963, and a doctorate from the University of Oregon in 1967. A longtime friend and colleague of his at the University of Colorado noted that he had written and published many articles in academic journals and was a devoted teacher. His wife said that her husband "very much liked to talk about economics."

Professor Schrock also had a strong interest in travel and teaching abroad. He participated in educational programs in several universities in the United Kingdom in the 1970s. The Office of Academic Affairs of the American Graduate School of International Management (Thunderbird), Thunderbird Campus in Glendale, Arizona noted in a memorandum that Schrock had returned to Arizona from Japan on Friday,

May 21. He had been in charge of a group of Thunderbird students in China and Japan since mid-December and had returned to handle routine administrative matters at the school before departing for a summer teaching program with Thunderbird at the Autonomous University of Guadalajara. As a part of his preparation, he received an advance from the university for his expenses in Mexico and purchased $5,000 in traveler's checks. In the early 1980s, while credit cards were accepted at major hotels and some tourist restaurants, most transactions – including buying gasoline – were handled with cash. To avoid carrying lots of cash, people purchased traveler's checks in U.S. dollars that could then be converted into Mexican pesos.

On May 30, Professor Schrock dropped his wife off at the Phoenix Sky Harbor International Airport so she could return to their home in Boulder, Colorado. Little did she know as she waved goodbye to him while boarding the plane that it would be the last time she would ever see him alive. Mrs. Schrock later said he was extremely excited over the anticipated summer in Guadalajara, not just because he loved teaching, but also as he planned extensive outdoor activities. Thunderbird colleagues that engaged with him after his return from Japan but before his departure to Mexico confirmed that he was in good spirits and ready for an enjoyable summer.

Professor Schrock's relatively new white 1981 Datsun four-wheel drive king cab pickup was jammed with camping, climbing, and hiking equipment as well as two cases of wine. It also contained a large amount of teaching materials for the school's use in its summer program, as well as someone's saxophone. His wife said that he was meticulous in keeping records such as driving distances and he delighted in consistently timing everything. He always had two watches with him, one a new digital model for timing and a dress watch.

According to information later given to the State Department by Thunderbird staff, on May 30, he telephoned a student while in Nogales, Arizona to discuss an assignment the student had not completed in the spring semester due to an illness. The student said that Professor Schrock remarked in passing that he was at Sanborn's Insurance Company in Nogales purchasing Mexican auto insurance.

According to his colleagues from Thunderbird, Schrock was due to arrive in Guadalajara on June 2, with his teaching duties to begin the following day. His colleagues at both Thunderbird and the University of Colorado said he was scrupulously punctual and would not have arrived late without a good reason. Dr. Marshall Geer, Vice President for Academic Affairs at Thunderbird, wrote in a note to his congressman regarding Professor Schrock's disappearance that he had known Schrock since 1957 and they had traveled together to Mexico several times previously. He later remarked that the Professor was an experienced traveler. While some colleagues said Schrock had a limited command of Spanish, Geer noted it was more than adequate for travel in Mexico.

When both Professor Schrock and another colleague failed to arrive on June 3, the director coordinating Thunderbird's program in Guadalajara and another colleague called the school in Arizona to see if Thunderbird officials had any information on the non-arrivals. On June 4, the wives of both professors were contacted, but neither had heard anything, and had not expected to be in contact with their husbands until several days later. Long distance calls at the time were relatively expensive, particularly international ones. The school's representatives said they sent a telex to the American Consulate General in Guadalajara indicating the two professors were overdue.

On Monday, June 7, officials from Thunderbird in Arizona called their colleagues in Guadalajara and learned that although the other professor arrived over the weekend, there was still no word regarding Professor Schrock. The officials in Guadalajara sent a telex to the American Consulate General in that city noting their strong concern regarding Schrock and requesting U.S. government assistance in locating him.

The next day, June 8, two senior officials from Thunderbird flew down to Guadalajara. While the visit had been arranged previously to handle routine matters related to the school's summer program, the search for Professor Schrock quickly became their top priority. They telephoned and had discussions with officials at the American Consulate General in Guadalajara who indicated they would be pursuing the matter, including sending out the initial welfare and whereabouts request the following morning. School officials also began calling a wider range of Mexican and U.S. officials over the next few days seeking assistance in the search and also began efforts to trace his route. They confirmed with Sanborn's in Nogales that Professor Schrock had indeed purchased auto insurance at that location on May 30.

The two Thunderbird officials flew back to Arizona where they also continued to seek assistance from law enforcement and other officials in the U.S. and Mexico. On Saturday June 12, they discovered the license plate number they had been using in the search, Colorado MR-3847, was incorrect. The right number was MR-3846. On Sunday, June 13, the first newspaper article on the disappearance appeared in a Boulder, Colorado newspaper.

On Monday, June 14, with Professor Schrock now almost two weeks overdue, Thunderbird officials sent additional information to their colleagues in Mexico including a passport picture of the Professor. They also began efforts to gain assistance from Arizona and Colorado's congressional delegations.

WEDNESDAY, JUNE 16 - THE SEARCH CONTINUES

Just as the staff of the Consular posts in Guadalajara, Hermosillo and Mazatlán were finishing up reporting on the results of their initial efforts, they began receiving additional information to aid in the search. The first of these was a June 16 cable from the Department of State in Washington that included information provided by Thunderbird officials regarding the Professor's credit card, passport and Mexican insurance. This message also confirmed the information that Consulate Hermosillo had previously reported that Professor Schrock had entered Mexico at Nogales on May 30. For the first time it also contained the license plate number MR-3846 and the serial number for the Professor's white Datsun pickup truck. It noted that a photo of Schrock would soon be provided to the three addressed Consulates. Interestingly, it did not include the Embassy in Mexico City as an addressee. It also ended with the helpful suggestion that we check with the Green Angels, hotels, hospitals, jails, morgues or funeral homes that we had already contacted.

This message from Washington said the offices of two members of Congress from Colorado, Rep. Timothy Worth and Sen. Bill Armstrong, were interested in this case. While it was not unusual for the Department to be contacted by congressional delegates regarding a particular consular matter, the fact that two offices had contacted the

Department so early was a bit unusual.

Before we heard about the disappearance of Professor Schrock, I had planned a trip north to Culiacán and Los Mochis for early July for prison visits and other consular business. There were several U.S. citizens imprisoned in the northern part of our consular districts that we visited periodically. Culiacán in particular had a large prison for convicted federal prisoners. We would also make visits to various hospitals, police offices and other locations likely to encounter Americans in trouble to strengthen our outreach network. Given that Professor Schrock was now more than two weeks overdue, we decided to accelerate the date for that trip and to include additional stops at jails, hotels and with Mexican officials to aid in the search. I, therefore, planned to leave the next day, Thursday, June 17, for the three-day round trip needed to reach Los Mochis in the far northern part of our district and to handle the various stops. We reported this decision and other search related matters to Washington and the other Mexican consular posts the following day. We also decided to similarly accelerate a consular visit to the southern part of our district by Vice Consul Michael Oreste shortly after my return from the north. Our June 17 message raised the issue with the Embassy in Mexico City and the State Department in Washington as to whether we should begin briefing the local press to aid in the search.

The following morning as I was driving north on the main highway to Culiacán, the Consulate received additional information from Consulate General Guadalajara provided by Dr. Geer, an official at Thunderbird. He noted that, based on his previous travels, the Professor may have spent the night in Hermosillo, Guaymas (possibly at the Guaymas Inn or another motel at the north end of town), or in Culiacán at the Hotel Tres Rios. Hotel Tres Rios was well known to the Consulate as we frequently stayed there during our travels to the north and where I planned to stay that night. It was not a standard hotel but rather a series of individual bungalows in a garden setting. While it was generally a peaceful locale, about six months after my June 1982 visit, there was a firefight between rival drug trafficking groups in the lobby that spread across the grounds. In the early 1980s the drug cartels were quite active in Sinaloa and often settled disputes over turf with guns. The message from Guadalajara also mentioned they were mailing the Consulates in Mazatlán and Hermosillo copies of photos of Professor Schrock to share with local police authorities. Things moved slowly in those days. Even after almost three weeks following his disappearance, we still did not have a recent photo of the Professor.

My 140-mile drive north to Culiacán was uneventful, although as always slightly nerve racking. The ancient government vehicle, a rusty old International Harvester Scout, managed the trip well, but the truck traffic was intense and the road was in poor condition. There were many potholes and portions of the road where the shoulder had been washed out. The vehicle also did not have any air conditioning and it was hot, dusty and humid in mid-June on the Pacific coast of Mexico. My first stop in Culiacán was at the prison where I spent a couple of hours visiting American citizens. I then stopped in at the central municipal jail and with the State Judicial Police to see if they had any news on Professor Schrock and to emphasize the importance of increasing their efforts to look for him.

My next stop was to check in at the Hotel Tres Rios to freshen up before further calls. Many businesses and companies in this part of Mexico, including government offices, used to close down during the middle of the day but reopened in the late afternoon. I had planned to make further stops after resting a bit. The hotel clerk said the Consulate had called that morning to see if the hotel had any record of Professor Schrock and they also showed me their registry book containing entries from all of May and up to the date in June. There were no entries that were even close to Nicholas Schrock. The cable from Guadalajara had mentioned that the Professor had stayed at that hotel on previous trips. The hotel staff also said that the Consulate had left a message for me to call and check in, which I had planned to do. Without cellphones we relied on landlines and would frequently call during travels to check in. Other than briefing me on the Guadalajara cable on Professor Schrock's previous travel, they had little to add besides letting me know who they had called that day in areas I was traveling to. I similarly briefed them on my lack of success and also discussed some consular matters regarding the prison visit.

By then it was time to press on. No rest for vice consuls. My next stop was of particular importance. I was going to drop in on one of the senior advisers to Sinaloa Governor Antonio Toledo Corro. The Governor had only taken office the previous year after spending two years as Federal Secretary for Agricultural Reform under President Jose Lopez Portillo who had served a single six-year term from 1981-1986. Most observers viewed Toledo Corro as a close friend of the President's and an important figure in the Party of the Institutional Revolution (PRI) which had governed Mexico since 1929. Vice consuls normally did not call on governors, so I cultivated senior advisers. In any event the governor and his advisers were well plugged into events in that part of Mexico and could focus additional resources on the search for Professor Schrock who, based on the information we had at the time, might have never even entered our Consular district. Still in cases like these, it is important to pursue as many avenues as possible.

I had met the senior adviser, Jose Ramon Fuentevilla, through his brother Luis Fuentevilla who owned a restaurant in Mazatlán. Luis had graduated at the same school that I had – the University of Texas at Austin – and had become a good friend. His brother, Jose Ramon, was not only close to the Governor, but also to the head of the state office of Hacienda, a powerful office combining the state treasury with many law enforcement agencies. Several months earlier when I first traveled to Culiacán as a new vice consul in Mexico, I had tried to secure an appointment with Jose Ramon using his brother's name but was blocked by his staff, so I just showed up at his office and said I was there to meet with him. His brother Luis later told me Jose Ramon was intrigued by my confidence. In any event, after waiting about half an hour that initial time, I was ushered in to see Jose Ramon and had the first of many interesting exchanges with him.

This visit was no different and after the normal half hour wait, I was invited in for coffee. Jose Ramon and I spent much of our time discussing politics. The federal elections, including that for president, were only a couple of weeks away. He was sure, as most observers were, that the PRI candidate, Miguel de le Madrid, would win. Finally, I raised the issue of the missing professor. To my surprise he not only seemed to be fully briefed on the case, but also said that the state government was increasing its efforts to find Schrock. He then called in two of his staff and introduced them to me (although I knew one from previous visits). He gave me their direct contact information and told me to call them anytime we needed additional assistance or information. These contacts proved extremely useful later, at least until they were forced to resign, so that stop was worth it if for nothing else than the staff's future help. With that I excused myself, as I always did, saying I knew how busy he was – which was true – and departed. I made a few more stops in Culiacán and then headed back to the hotel to check in with the office and call it a day.

On Friday, June 18, I was up early to try to beat the heat in my 135-mile drive north to Los Mochis. The road was in somewhat better shape except for the last stretch from Guasave to Los Mochis, which required very slow going due to the poor state of the pavement. It was still extremely warm and dusty and there was heavy truck traffic. I stopped in Guasave enroute from Culiacán to talk to the police and officials in the mayor's office to make sure they were aware of the missing professor. I made similar stops in Los Mochis but added a visit to the prison and to a meeting with a group of businessmen from the Chamber of Commerce. I also checked with several hotels to raise awareness about the missing professor. By then it was after 9 p.m., so after checking in with acting Principal Officer Ron Kramer at the Consulate in Mazatlán, I called it a day.

On Saturday, June 19, after a few more stops, I began the 270-mile drive back to Mazatlán. While the trip was long, dusty, hot and with heavy traffic, I managed to make it back to Mazatlán by midafternoon. Along the route I stopped and spoke with toll booth collectors asking them if they had heard of Professor Schrock's disappearance, news of which was just beginning to appear in the local press. I was also constantly looking for white pickup trucks. En route, just north of Mazatlán, a bridge was closed for repair, as it had been in my trip north, and I had to go down a detour over a bumpy, steep dirt hill across a ditch and up the other side. I remember thinking that this would be a good place to try to rob someone as they had to drive very slowly and there was little traffic, at least during the time I drove through there.

Over the next week, each of the Consulates reported its ongoing efforts with little new information. Mazatlán's Vice Consul Oreste drove down to Tepic, Nayarit to meet with local police, immigration and prison officials, the Governor's Office, hotels and hospitals. At Mazatlán's request, consular officers from Guadalajara volunteered to drive to San Blas to investigate a report of the deaths of two American citizens. They quickly identified one of the victims as an American citizen, but not Professor Schrock. The other victim was much younger than the Professor and had a long ponytail. He was later identified as a U.S. citizen.

Washington was also supplying additional information during that third week of June, such as Professor Schrock having two cases of wine in his truck. The Department also cabled numerous questions, such as asking the consular posts in Mexico to confirm whether there was an aircraft search being conducted by Mexican officials – there was not. Following up on Consulate Mazatlán's June 17 cabled suggestion regarding reaching out to the press, a message from Washington stated that Mrs. Schrock would like the U.S. missions in Mexico to prepare and release newspaper ads with Professor Schrock's photo, which posts had still not received. Mrs. Schrock indicated she would pay for the ads. The Embassy and posts began coordinating the text of those ads as they waited for the photos to arrive by airmail. The State Department's messages also reported that eight congressional offices were now interested in this welfare and whereabouts case including Congressmen Timothy Wirth (Colorado) and Ken Kramer (Colorado), Congresswoman Millicent Fenwick (New Jersey) as well as Senators William Armstrong (Colorado), Barry Goldwater (Arizona), Jake Garn (Utah), Gary Hart (Colorado) and Dennis DeConcini (Arizona).

MONDAY, JUNE 28
- THE TRUCK

Monday, June 28th started as most days did at the Consulate in Mazatlán. We were at work early, largely processing non-immigrant visas and handling other routine consular matters. Our staff was also continuing to make calls across our consular district regarding Professor Schrock. As I had been having mechanical trouble with my personal vehicle, which due to the press of work I hadn't been able to remedy, I took an early lunch to take the car over to a local repair shop to get it looked at. At about 11:30 a.m., while waiting at the dealership, I was approached by a familiar-looking man who asked if I was Vice Consul Downes. As consular officers have the power to issue non-immigrant visas, we were widely known and it was not unusual to be approached in this manner. In fact, I was often at restaurants in rural areas I had not visited before and would be greeted by the waiter with, "What would the vice consul like to order?"

In any event, I confirmed my identity and asked him how I could help him. I thought at the time it was just a chance encounter, but later learned that he had deliberately followed me from the Consulate so he wouldn't be seen talking to me there. While he wouldn't give me his name, he said he was an employee of State Gobernación (a state agency with administrative and law enforcement responsibilities, including the recovery of stolen vehicles) and asked if I was looking for a white pickup truck. I admitted I was and that it had Colorado license plates "MR- ..." He interrupted me to continue "... 3846." Without any prodding from me, he then went on to verify a general description of the vehicle, a white four-wheel drive pickup truck. The man then said that the truck had been found abandoned along the main Mazatlán-to-Culiacán highway around June 9 and was in the possession of the municipal police in San Ignacio. While the description exactly matched the Professor's truck, the date seemed wrong. The source said that Fausto Medina of State Gobernación in Culiacán would have further details. With that, the man turned and departed.

Then everything happened at once. I abandoned, yet again, my efforts to get my car repaired and immediately returned to the Consulate where, in rapid succession, the following transpired. I alerted acting Principal Officer Ron Kramer and the rest of the staff to my discovery. Kramer and Vice Consul Oreste called the Embassy in Mexico City and the State Department's Operations Center in Washington to let them know we might have found the truck. We also sent a short cable to Washington and all the relevant Consular posts in Mexico regarding the new information on the truck and indicating we would travel to San Ignacio that day to further investigate. I also called Fausto Medina Alvarado, the Sub-Director of Gobernación whose office was in the Palacio de Gobierno (the main state government complex) in Culiacán. I had met Medina on a previous visit to Culiacán in May, and while we had spoken to other officials in his office regarding the search for Professor Schrock, we had not talked directly with him. Medina verified that the missing vehicle was indeed in the custody of the municipal police in

San Ignacio but could not explain why the Consulate had not been notified of the discovery. Medina then said to be very careful in traveling to San Ignacio as "it was a dangerous place." He noted that discovery of the truck had been routinely reported to Gobernación, but not to the Consulate itself as the local police wanted to use it for their own purposes. I replied that we would be heading to San Ignacio that afternoon and said we should talk further the next day.

As we had been warned about the danger of travel to San Ignacio, I called a friend who worked for the Mexico-United States Commission for Screwworm Eradication. This was a bilateral commission run by the U.S. Department of Agriculture and its Mexican counterpart to try to control a pest that damaged the cattle industry. My colleague frequently traveled to extremely remote areas of Mexico and knew the country well. I was able to reach him at once and he confirmed that San Ignacio was indeed "a dangerous area due to drug trafficking" and to be very careful. He suggested that we check in with the Mexican army which had a small detachment in that city.

San Ignacio is a scenic, old colonial-style town that lies roughly 65 miles north of Mazatlán. It is on Highway 6, a narrow two-lane road that runs from Highway 15, the InterAmerican Highway and the main road between Culiacán and Mazatlán, for 25 miles north up into the mountains where the road terminates at San Ignacio. Due to the poor condition of the road, it was about an hour and 45-minute drive from the Consulate. Vice Consul Oreste and I departed as soon as we could in the other of the Consulate's elderly vehicles, an old Ford four-door sedan, to head up to San Ignacio, a town neither of us had had reason to visit previously. As we crossed the picturesque old bridge over the Rio Ajoya, we were not enjoying the view, but rather planning our next steps.

Our first stop was with the local army detachment. We identified ourselves to the lieutenant on duty and explained why we were in San Ignacio. He indicated that he had seen the truck being driven by the police but had no additional information. We told him that we were going to meet with the police, but if we were not back in an hour, to please come and check on us.

We then proceeded to the local municipal offices, which were closed for the afternoon. A policeman on duty directed us to the house of Jose Luis Tapia Rueda Flores who was the representative of the state office of the Ministerio Publico (an office whose responsibilities include judicial and prosecutorial issues) in San Ignacio which would handle missing vehicles. Tapia told us that the truck had been discovered by the police near the main highway on June 7, apparently abandoned with the keys in it. (That date still appeared to Mike and me as far too late given theProfessor's travel plans.) Apparently, even though San Ignacio was 25 miles north of the main highway, that city's municipal police had jurisdiction over a section of the highway, including that portion where the truck was found. Normally an abandoned vehicle would be turned over to the control of Tapia's ministry, but the police chief and the mayor (Presidente Municipal), Francisco Javier Palacios Sarabia, had decided to keep the vehicle for their own purposes. He further added that he had sent a telegram to his superiors in Culiacán on June 9 informing them of the situation.

Tapia agreed to accompany us to the police station. There

we had the officer on duty radio the police chief who said he would return with the policeman who had discovered the vehicle and accompany us to the site where the vehicle was found. While waiting for the police chief, at our request, the policeman on duty showed us a room containing roughly 12 cardboard boxes and two bags of materials that he said had been found in the truck. He would not let us inspect the material closely until the police chief arrived, but when he did, a short inspection revealed name tags of "Nicholas Schrock" on the luggage. We had found at least some trace of the Professor.

Before the police chief arrived, we also asked the policeman on duty to give us a tour of the police station and its outbuildings, including two holding cells. We said we had a great interest in police work and rural operations, but we really just wanted to ensure Professor Schrock, or someone with knowledge of his disappearance, was not there. All cells were empty, and the policeman said they hadn't arrested anyone recently.

About that time, we again sent word back to the army base in San Ignacio and requested their assistance in searching the area where the vehicle was found. In the meantime, someone -- not the police chief -- drove up in a white Datsun pickup. The police had removed the license plates and the temporary Mexican importation sticker, but we were quickly able to confirm with the serial number that it was Professor Schrock's vehicle. It also had an April 1982 Colorado inspection sticker. The driver told us that when the truck was found it had gas; all the tires were in good shape; and it ran well. This made it unlikely that the Professor's truck had broken down. We inspected the truck and indeed found it in extremely good condition. The other thing that was interesting was that on both sides of the car were large campaign posters for the PRI, the ruling party in Mexico. They had been using the truck as a part of the political efforts for July 4 national elections.

Shortly thereafter the chief of police arrived. As it was growing late, after a brief inspection of the possessions found in the truck, we decided our time was better spent searching the area where the vehicle was found. We could return to inspect the materials found in the truck the next day. The police chief also said the police had traveler's checks and other papers from the truck stored elsewhere in the building. Even though it was just past the summer solstice when days are quite lengthy in the United States, Mazatlán lies just south of the Tropic of Cancer so the length of the day doesn't vary as much and it was growing dark. So we set off accompanied by an agent from the public ministry, the police chief and six of his officers, and a Mexican army lieutenant with about a dozen of his soldiers.

According to the police, the truck was found about 35 miles from San Ignacio on the main highway, just about 35 miles north of Mazatlán. To be more exact, it was on a dirt road 100 yards from the main highway at what the police added was at mile point 37. It was also less than a mile on the Mazatlán side of the detour that I had noted as a potential robbery site on my drive back to Mazatlán the week before. At the site we found several empty cartons which had apparently been mailed to Professor Schrock by priority mail in care of the Arizona campus of Thunderbird, supporting the police assertion that the truck had once been there. We also found several broken wine or champagne bottles. By this time it was dark. The army lieutenant agreed to meet us at the site the following morning at 8 a.m. to continue the search.

Vice Consul Oreste and I drove back to the Consulate in Mazatlán where we were shortly thereafter met by Ronald Kramer, the acting Principal Officer. We spent the next two hours calling the Embassy in Mexico City and the Operations Center at the State Department in Washington reporting what we had learned that day and in drafting a detailed message to Washington, the Embassy and the relevant Consulates which was sent out the following morning. In the message, the Consulate also recommended the Embassy file a diplomatic protest with the Mexican government for the lack of notification of the truck which had cost valuable weeks in the search for the missing professor. We also raised serious doubts as to some of the statements made by the San Ignacio police. And before calling it a night, we reviewed cables from Consulate Hermosillo reporting a number of new leads they had received as a result of the newspaper and television reports that had appeared in Sonora.

TUESDAY, JUNE 29 – THE SEARCH FOR THE BODY

As Vice Consul Oreste was needed for other duties, I was directed to return to the north to continue the search alone. My first objective was a more thorough examination of the site where the truck was found and secondly to try to search and possibly recover Professor Schrock's possessions and/or his truck. Departing early, I arrived at the site where the vehicle was supposedly found. Now that it was daylight, I could see that the site was 100 yards west of the highway and near the 59-kilometer highway marker, not the 37-mile marker that the police gave. At about 8:15 a.m. I was met by Lieutenant Jesus Marques with 14 soldiers from the Mexican army base in San Ignacio. I asked the lieutenant if he had had much experience in searching for bodies and he smiled and replied, "Some." He suggested we begin a grid search covering an area significantly larger than the immediate area, which we did. The soldiers did a good job taking the search seriously and were quite thorough. Perhaps they were glad with the change in routine. I also personally walked and examined the entire search area including small heavy wooded ravines on both sides of the flat open area where the vehicle was allegedly found.

About 10 a.m. we were joined by three heavily armed individuals who identified themselves as being law enforcement officials from the Sinoloan Gobernación and from the State Judicial Police. They pulled me aside and said the governor "was concerned with my safety as this was a very dangerous place to be alone." I responded that I was fine as I was "with my friends, the Mexican army." I found out later that Vice Consul Oreste had made some follow-up calls to the Governor's Office in Culiacán and mentioned in passing his concern for my safety. The governor was out of town, but one of his special secretaries, Luis Pena Farber, took the point and sent his agents to aid in the search. Since it was clear that everyone knew I was there and the army had provided strong cooperation, I did not feel threatened on June 29 as I had on the previous day when the police had been openly hostile to our visit and when I was glad we had checked in with the Army. The agents watched from the shade while the soldiers and I continued to search the area.

After about three-and-a-half hours, we finished the grid search but found no additional traces that Professor Schrock might have once been there. It was towards the end of the dry season and the earth was baked and almost rock-hard. We didn't find any soil that looked recently disturbed, but had Professor Schrock been there, he had been so for almost a month earlier and the ground had hardened. There were also four small ranches within five miles of the site but questioning of their residents added no further information. We, therefore, decided to end the search and proceed to San Ignacio. I told the lieutenant I would check in with him before I left his city and thanked him and his men for their assistance. He responded that they would be happy to help further should we want to search this site again or another site.

When we got to San Ignacio, the three state law

enforcement agents from Culiacán essentially told the mayor and the chief of police to load all of the Professor's possessions in the Professor's truck as they were going to drive it to Mazatlán to turn over to the Consulate. After a moment or two of pained silence, the mayor directed that it be done. This was a bit unusual as we normally took possession of stolen or missing vehicles belonging to U.S. citizens by filing a written petition with the state public ministry and signing a long document outlining the facts. Given the importance of the search and the Mexican police's failure to follow normal procedure, I was not about to insist on routine.

I decided that rather than conduct a thorough examination of the possessions and the truck in San Ignacio, since I unexpectedly had an opportunity to have them turned over to the Consulate, I would delay an examination until they were in our control. I still insisted on a thorough search of the site for anything that might have been forgotten and again to see if there were any prisoners that might be questioned. The police chief handed the traveler's checks and other personal papers directly to me and I signed a written receipt for them as was standard practice.

Before leaving, and in the presence of the state law enforcement officers, I questioned the police in more detail about their previous responses pointing out several inconsistencies in their statements the day before. They admitted that they had taken possession of the vehicle on June 3, rather than June 7. Other than that, they provided evasive answers and had little to add. After saying goodbye to the Army, I left San Ignacio with my new Culiacán-based colleagues.

One of the Culiacán-based agents drove the truck to the Consulate in Mazatlán, with the second following in their vehicle. The third insisted on riding back with me "for my safety." He spent most of the time on the drive back playing with the car radio or making comments about his colleagues driving abilities. It was a quick trip as the lead driver drove quite quickly and I did not want to lose sight of the truck. Once we arrived at the Consulate, the driver of the truck handed me the keys and, after promising the full efforts of the Governor of Sinaloa to aid in the search, he and his colleagues departed.

Although we spent some time reporting to the Embassy and the State Department by telephone and writing yet another long cable outlining the day's events, our highest priority was to carefully examine the truck and its possessions to see if they would shed any further light on Professor Schrock's disappearance. The first thing we noted was what looked like rust-colored stains on the passenger seat and floor of the front seat. They looked like they might be blood. The car radio also appeared to have been slightly damaged as if someone had tried to remove it. The lower dashboard on the passenger side of the car was also damaged--again as if someone had tried to pry it open. Other than that, the truck appeared to be in good shape and we moved it into the Consulate's crowded one-car garage, the alternative being to leave it out on the street in front of the Consulate as we had no other dedicated protected parking space.

Professor Schrock's driving logbook was in one of the boxes of materials, but only contained the information that he bought a total of 165 liters of gasoline at four stops. The mileage and locations were not included. The odometer read 12,942.6 miles when it arrived at the Consulate in Mazatlán, indicating the car had traveled 1,357 miles since its last fill up before crossing the border in Nogales, at least according to Professor Schrock's notebook. For reference, the driving distance from Nogales to Mazatlán was about 730 miles, at the time along the old Culiacan-Mazatlán stretch which has since been rerouted and modernized. Since the San Ignacio police had been driving the vehicle since June 3, this information was of less use in determining if the Professor had made any side trips.

As we sorted through his possessions, it appeared that Professor Schrock had originally put most things in knapsacks and duffel bags. The police in San Ignacio had repacked them into boxes in a very haphazard manner, making it more difficult to sort through them. The police also were not as thorough in their search as we were as we found $100 in cash in one small zipper compartment. We also found the Colorado license plates, the Mexican car import sticker issued in Nogales, and his Mexican insurance policy. We reported the denominations and serial numbers of the $370 in travel's checks we found among the Professor's papers to the concerned agencies in our report.

An important find during the initial look at the materials was a Bancomer (credit card processing bank) receipt indicating that Professor Schrock spent the night of May 30, 1982, at the Hotel Gandara, in Hermosillo, Sonora. We immediately called the Consulate in that city, and they subsequently verified that information with the hotel. That overnight stop agreed with our understanding of his intended travel plans. The 550 mile or 11- to 13-hour drive from Hermosillo to Mazatlán on the old highway meant he would be in the Mazatlán area at the earliest sometime late on June 1, or at the latest June 2 assuming he stopped somewhere enroute on the night of May 31.

Professor Schrock's passport was also among those documents given to me by the police chief in San Ignacio. It did not contain any entry stamps for Mexico, but at the time you did not need a U.S. passport to travel between the two countries, only a tourist card issued at the border. We did not find Professor Schrock's tourist card, nor did we find his wallet.

While I was in San Ignacio that morning, two men identifying themselves as agents from Mexico's Dirección Federal de Seguridad (DFS) arrived unannounced at the Consulate in Mazatlán. The Federal Security Directorate, while having similar powers and responsibilities to that of the U.S. Federal Bureau of Investigation, was quite notorious. The DFS was widely accused during the 1970s of participating in criminal activities and human rights abuses. It was finally disbanded in 1985 by the Mexican Minister of Interior. In any event, DFS agents were then active in Western Mexico. The agents said they were acting on a request for assistance from the American Consulate in Hermosillo. They had little information to share but were fully briefed by Consulate staff and departed promising additional assistance.

In response to our initial short cable the day before informing Washington that we had a tip on the location on the vehicle, we received a short message indicating that according to Mrs. Schrock, Professor Schrock always kept a logbook (which we had already located) in his glove compartment to monitor his mileage. She also asked what she needed to do to have the truck transferred back to the United States. This case is a bit unusual in that we had not formally taken possession of the truck from the Mexican government. As I noted earlier, in previous cases we generally did so by making a written demand on the relevant state officials. We suggested the Embassy might be better suited to answer that question. Mrs. Schrock also said she thought we ought to try to find some search dogs, although she noted the trail was probably cold. The cable went on to report that she said she was prepared to hire another private investigator, a matter with which she said she would discuss directly with the Consulate in Mazatlán rather than with the Department. She later raised the issue with us.

WEDNESDAY, JUNE 30 - GEORGIA SHERIFFS

In our daily missive regarding the search for Professor Schrock to Washington and to the Embassy in Mexico City on Wednesday, June 30, the Consulate noted the rising interest in the case by the U.S. press. We particularly reported various journalists calling the Consulate identifying themselves as being from the *Denver Post* and *Rocky Mountain News* and quoting verbatim from the Mazatlán cable reporting on the June 28 search for the vehicle. We generally did not talk directly with journalists regarding welfare and whereabouts cases in order to protect the privacy of the U.S. citizens involved. Instead, we usually referred journalists, as we were instructed to do, to the press section of the U.S. Embassy in Mexico City. We certainly did not release the text of our cables, and always worked to protect the privacy of U.S. citizens in distress.

About this time two incidents involving the press transpired and caused us major heartburn over the following weeks. The first was quite troubling. The residence of the U.S. Consul was vacant as the Consul had departed and we were expecting the imminent arrival of his successor. Acting Principal Officer Ron Kramer was living in a short-term apartment rental. Two representatives of the U.S. press talked their way past the Mexican police guard at the empty residence. They then set up shop there and began answering the phone as if they were Consulate employees. Although they apparently did not learn anything useful regarding the disappearance of Professor Schrock, they did learn private information from several of our other Consulate cases, including a death case. The following day as soon as we learned of their presence, we had the police escort them out of the building and increased the security there. These were American journalists from well-respected organizations pursuing their work in a fashion that most reporters would consider dishonorable.

As the Consulate reported the following day, most of our efforts on June 30 were spent examining and inventorying all of Professor Schrock's possessions, everything from wool socks to Windex. All items were carefully inspected, reviewed and repacked. Although the inventory was completed June 30, it wasn't typed up and formally signed until Friday, July 2 when copies were also mailed to Mrs. Schrock and the U.S. Embassy in Mexico City. Little additional evidence was found, although it was clear that a number of items he had with him were missing, including a small radio. One thing we noticed in particular was that although he was supposed to have brought lots of clothing with him, we didn't inventory nearly as much as we expected to find.

We also took another closer look at Professor Schrock's driving log, which was difficult to read. It did indicate the truck got roughly 22 miles per gallon and that he had purchased 110 liters (about 29 gallons) in three stops of 55, 20 and 35, and not the 165 liters we originally reported. Barring long side trips, he likely made his third stop for gasoline near Culiacán about 615 miles from Nogales, Sonora where he entered Mexico.

The Consulate was also in telephone contact with Consulate Hermosillo whose staff was following up with the hotel in that city. They subsequently reported that the Hotel Gandara confirmed the hotel registry showed a Nicholas Schrock with the Department of Economics in Boulder, Colorado. The Professor paid using a credit card and apparently departed before 10 a.m. on May 31 as he was not in his room when the maid checked it for cleaning purposes. No one in the hotel or its dining room recognized him from his picture. The hotel staff said the Mexican police had also visited the hotel asking the same questions. The hotel bill totaled 1,210 pesos, including tax, equivalent to about $25 at the exchange rate at the time. Those messages also reported on Consulate Hermosillo's continued efforts to find information regarding the missing professor.

The Embassy in Mexico City also notified the Consulates that Embassy staff had provided the numbers of the missing traveler's checks to the American Express office in Mexico City asking that the Embassy be notified immediately if any of these were cashed. That same day Ambassador Gavin phoned and spoke with Sinoloan Governor Antonio Toledo Corro and urged that all necessary action be taken to locate Professor Schrock and to call into account the officials in San Ignacio for their actions in hindering the search for the Professor.

It seems like a lot was packed into the day, although less than the previous two, but it was not over. After spending the day closely checking over Professor Schrock's vehicle and possessions and transmitted the necessary reports by cable and telephone, we were taking a quiet moment in the Consul's office to discuss our next moves. The phone rang and acting Principal Officer Kramer answered it. It was a stringer from the Associated Press asking about reports that Professor Schrock's truck was found. Kramer had it on speaker phone so I could clearly hear both sides of the conversation. The reporter apparently had access to quite a bit of information that was not public which the Consulate had transmitted to Washington and Mexico City regarding the recovery of the truck. This included such items as the extra $100 in cash found along with other items.

Kramer confirmed that the vehicle was positively identified as that of the Professor and that it had been located in San Ignacio in the possession of the municipal police but added little more than that. The reporter then said something like, "So what is a police chief like in San Ignacio? Is it like a Georgia sheriff, with a pot belly and mirrored sunglasses?" Unfortunately, at that point Kramer said something like, "Mirrored sunglasses--no not at all. I don't think you can make that comparison." He never agreed with the assertion or mentioned the state of Georgia. They talked several more minutes but nothing noteworthy was added to the conversation.

The next day an Associated Press article appeared in a Colorado newspaper and was picked up by the *Atlanta Journal Constitution* in its July 2, 1982, edition. The article contained numerous inaccuracies. For example, it indicated the police chief drove up in the truck to meet the consular officers. It quoted extensively from Alan Romberg, identified as State Department Deputy Press Spokesman. It also, unfortunately, quoted from Acting Principal Officer Ron Kramer and falsely attributed the reporter's derogatory and stereotypical remarks to Kramer. Specifically, it read in part:

> It sort of reminds you of those Georgia sheriffs with a pot belly and mirrored glasses," said Ronald Kramer, temporary U.S. Consul.

As one can imagine, as a result of this misattribution, Consulate Mazatlán, the Embassy in Mexico City and the State Department in Washington spent much of the next four months responding to outraged correspondence, including some addressed to the U.S. Secretary of State, from the entire Congressional delegation of Georgia, candidates running for office in Georgia, the Georgia Sheriff's Association, the National Sheriff's Association (which wrote directly to President Ronald Reagan), various other Georgia law enforcement agencies and a number of citizens of that great state. I truly understand the concerns of the writers, but responding to this reporter's misattribution used up substantial U.S. government resources that might have better been used elsewhere. I am a strong advocate for transparency and providing the press as much non-private information as possible, but there are dangers in talking openly with some reporters.

Thursday, July 1, 1982, began like most days with early morning consular work. The seasonal non-immigrant visa load in Mazatlán was at its peak meaning the number of Mexicans applying to visit the United States was high. Each application required an interview and careful adjudication. This was in the months leading up to the first peso crisis. Although the peso had been devalued in February, it was still overvalued compared to the U.S. dollar and thus many middle-class Mexican citizens could afford to travel to the United States to visit such attractions as Disneyland in California. The peso would begin its major collapse in a matter of weeks.

We also continued our efforts to pressure federal, state and local Mexican authorities to increase their efforts to find Professor Schrock. That day we received two messages from Washington that appeared to have been delayed in transit. The first clarified that Mrs. Schrock was not pressing for immediate return of the vehicle, at least not before an exhaustive series of tests were performed. We were already in direct contact with Mrs. Schrock by telephone and she was, while frustrated with the lack of progress, always direct and helpful. I spoke with her later that day regarding the testing of the rust-colored stains in the car. She gave us clear, although verbal, permission to remove whatever portions of the seat and flooring were necessary for forensic tests. I told her – and we also reported to the State Department and the U.S. Embassy in Mexico City – that "increasing interest in the stains is perhaps generating more interest than is warranted." I wrote, "The stains in question are of the faintest variety and could well be a myriad of substances besides blood." We were working with the Embassy and Washington to try to find the appropriate agency or lab to examine the stains.

There was, in fact, heightened press interest in the blood stains in particular and the disappearance of Professor Schrock in general. One example is a series of articles by Mike Stone of the *Rocky Mountain News* of Denver, Colorado. In an article headlined, "Stains accelerate search for CU prof" and published Friday, July 2, 1982, he noted:

An intensified search for missing University of Colorado economics professor Nicholas Schrock had been launched after suspected blood stains were found inside the cab of his truck.

Later in the article he accurately quoted me (as he had in all of his articles) in a passage that read:

> U.S. consulate officials in Mazatlán are awaiting word on where to send the samples from the three small stains.
>
> Vice Consul Robert Downes said Thursday that the stains "may be blood. They're small and faint and could possibly be from rusty water or something like that."
>
> He said the stains are each about half the size of a dime. One stain was found on the passenger seat, one between the seats, and one on the floor. He said the consulate is awaiting clarification for the U.S. Embassy in Mexico City on where to send the samples. "We won't have them evaluated in Mazatlán," Downes said. "They'll either go to Mexico City or back to the states."

When I spoke with Mrs. Schrock that day, she also expressed an interest in visiting Mazatlán and San Ignacio. I assured her that if she did so, the Consulate's staff would assist her with the visit. I was very careful though to not lead her to believe that her presence would necessarily develop new information. I frankly did not want to raise false hopes, but also didn't want to discourage her from coming if she decided to. She said she would notify us immediately of her travel plans if she decided to come.

The first message from Washington mentioned above asked if the saxophone of Professor Schrock had been located. We replied that it had not and was, to my knowledge, never found. The cable also reminded post (referring to the Consulate in Mazatlán) that about $5,000 of traveler's checks were still unaccounted for, something we were aware of and confirmed in a cable later that day. The missing traveler's checks, except for the $370 we received from the San Ignacio Police, were never found nor am I aware of any efforts to cash them.

The second cable from Washington said the State Department agreed with Consulate Mazatlán's earlier suggestion that the Embassy make a formal protest of the lack of notification from Mexican authorities after they found the Professor's missing vehicle. It also confirmed that officials at the State Department had not released any of post's reporting cables to the press. They did note that our cable reporting the June 28 discovery of the vehicle had been read to Mrs. Schrock over the phone.

We later learned that on July 1 that the U.S. Embassy in Mexico City had issued its first press release on the case in English and Spanish. The State Department issued similar guidance at the noon press briefing in Washington. The Mexico City statement read:

U.S Ambassador to Mexico John Gavin and other Embassy Officials have been in contact with Mexican officials at the national and state levels regarding the case of an American citizen who disappeared in Mexico last month.

Professor Nicholas Schrock crossed the border on May 30 en route to Guadalajara, but never arrived. U.S. Embassy officials spent hundreds of hours trying to find Professor

Schrock. Earlier this week, his vehicle and some of his belongings were located by U.S. Consular officials near San Ignacio, in the State of Sinaloa.

Ambassador Gavin spoke with the Governor of the State of Sinaloa, Antonio Toledo Corro, to communicate the interest of the U.S. Government in the investigation.

The Ambassador has been aware of this case and concerned about it since it was reported to him in early June.

Later that afternoon the Consulate in Mazatlán sent in a long cable that reported the events of the day outlined above. It also contained a plea for additional assistance, noting the heavy non-immigrant visa load and the steadily increasing number of media officials contacting the Consulate by phone or arriving in person. The volume of interest in this case, combined with our continuing telephone probes of Mexican officials, was beginning to become a problem. We were also missing a number of routine, yet important, reporting and administrative deadlines. (The Embassy quickly gave us leave to complete a number of nonessential items well after their normal due dates.)

Our outgoing cable noted that Acting Principal Officer Kramer was returning to his post in Monterrey, Mexico on July 10 and the new Principal Officer, Elayne Urban, was to arrive in Mazatlán the following day. We urged the Embassy to fully brief Consul Urban when she arrived in Mexico City before traveling to Mazatlán. With that we called it a day.

FRIDAY, JULY 2 - A BODY FOUND?

The day did not begin auspiciously. Our telex machine was not working, making it impossible to send or receive diplomatic messages, so in addition to our normal workload, we spent substantial time on the phone with the State Department and Embassy to ensure that we were not missing anything important. It was necessary to maintain fairly constant contact given the fast nature of developments in this and other consular matters.

While the telex was out, we also continued to trade information with Mexican federal officials by phone and to encourage them to take additional steps to search for Professor Schrock. Mexican federal agents from DFS reported that they had questioned local authorities and other witnesses in San Ignacio. They said that Professor Schrock's truck was seen on June 2, 1982, by a passing bus driver at the location the police indicated they found it. The bus driver notified his union, which contacted the police in San Ignacio. Evidently it was so late in the afternoon on June 2 that the police waited until the morning of June 3 to drive down to the InterAmerican Highway and take possession of the vehicle.

Consulate officials also discussed the case with Roberto Robles Rendon, Director of the Dirección de Seguridad Pública Municipal (Municipal Police Chief) in Culiacán. He said Governor Toledo Corro had requested that he assist in the case. He told us that there had been some reports of individuals stopping cars and robbing their occupants between Culiacán and Mazatlán, including on the highway near San Ignacio. Men in cars would reportedly stop other vehicles claiming to be plainclothes federal police, he said. They would then rob the occupants at gunpoint but would allow the victims to continue on their way. The Culiacán police had not previously reported any such problems to the Consulate, nor had we had any reports of U.S. citizens being robbed in this manner.

Robles Rendon also said they had arrested a man with traveler's checks and a Rolex watch on June 9. He suggested this man might have robbed Professor Schrock. On further questioning he admitted the checks were not from American Express as Professor Schrock's were. Nor did the Professor have a Rolex. We were constantly getting reports of possible arrests or sightings, but the great majority, after only cursory additional questioning, appeared erroneous.

Once the telex began to work, we submitted a long cable reporting on our day's efforts. We also received a Guadalajara cable updating Senator Gary Hart on the Embassy's and Consulates' efforts to find Professor Schrock. Washington thoughtfully sent us a cable indicating that now seventeen U.S. senators and congressmen were interested in the search for Professor Schrock. It also noted that Dr. Geer of Thunderbird had located dental X-rays for Professor Schrock which were available if needed. He also confirmed that the Professor's blood type was O positive. Both data points would be needed should we locate a body.

It was now 6 p.m. on a Friday evening. It had been a

very long week in finding the truck, searching the field, going through Professor Schrock's possessions for anything that might help us search for him, and dealing with the press. We decided that enough had been done and we headed home hoping for a more normal weekend, particularly as Sunday was the Fourth of July. It was not to be.

At 7:20 p.m., Acting Principal Officer Kramer received a call at his temporary apartment from the Governor of Sinaloa, Antonio Toledo Corro. The governor notified Kramer that Professor Schrock had been assaulted and murdered near Coyotitán, a small town about ten kilometers north of the place where his Datsun pickup had been sighted on the evening of June 2. The governor expressed his great concern and regret over the matter. He added that Mexican officials had one suspect in custody and were seeking a second individual. He said that his office would make a formal notification to the Embassy the next day but wanted Mr. Kramer to notify Ambassador Gavin as soon as possible. Kramer thanked the Governor for his prompt notification and cooperation and said he would ensure that the Ambassador was informed.

Acting Principal Officer Kramer then called Howard Jackson, the Press Attaché for the Embassy in Mexico City, briefed him and asked him to brief the Ambassador. Then he contacted Vice Consul Oreste and me and told us what was up. From home, I immediately called Roberto Robles Rendon, Chief of Police in Culiacán, and separately another special aide to Gov. Toledo Corro. Both men confirmed that agents of Gobernación (state police) and DFS had questioned individuals up and down the Culiacán-Mazatlán highway and had become suspicious of a gas station attendant who "at length" admitted his part in the crime and implicated his accomplices.

Robles Rendon then added that at that time (about 8 p.m. on Friday evening), the suspect and police officials were enroute to the site where he expected the body of Professor Schrock to be found. No body had yet been found. Despite repeated questions regarding the location where the body was supposed to be, Robles Rendon was extremely vague. He said he would call me when he had further information. I then contacted the operation center in Washington, D.C. to update them on the case, including the Governor's call with Kramer. I also called Howard Jackson in Mexico City to let him know what I had learned.

By this time Ambassador Gavin had notified the principals in the case and I soon received calls from Mrs. Schrock and Dr. Geer from Thunderbird routed to me from the operations center in Washington, D.C. (although both individuals had my home phone number). They said that both Mrs. Schrock and Dr. Geer would travel to Mazatlán the next day and provided us with their preliminary travel information. Mrs. Schrock said she wanted to be the first to view the corpse and stated she would bring Professor Schrock's dental record for positive identification. She added that it was her wish that once positively identified, the remains be immediately cremated. I cautioned her that, based on the information available, the Mexican police only had a suspect and not, repeat, not a body. I also said we would arrange for her to be met the next morning when she arrived.

I then spoke with Ron Kramer and Vice Consul Oreste and we agreed that I would get up early and try to find the police search party and one or both of them would meet Mrs.

Schrock and Dr. Geer. Mrs. Schrock must have immediately contacted the press because about 10:25 p.m. Kramer received a call from the *Denver Post*'s reporter in Mazatlán, Mr. Kit Miniclier, whom we had all met earlier and was in Mexico at the time. Mr. Miniclier was aware of details which only someone who had spoken with the Ambassador would have known. That said, we had a very good relationship with Mr. Miniclier who consistently acted in a professional manner throughout the case.

SATURDAY, JULY 3 - A SEARCH FOR THE SEARCH

At first light I drove out of Mazatlán to attempt to verify the reports that the body of Professor Schrock had been found. It was a hot and humid morning, and you could feel that the rainy season would soon be with us. Just before 6 a.m., I arrived at the site where the police said they had found the truck. There was no sign of a search or any other activity underway. In fact, it was very quiet with little traffic passing along the highway. After waiting a few minutes, I decided to proceed north along the highway as the Culiacán police had only said they were searching "in the area" where the truck was found abandoned. I drove for about twenty kilometers (12 miles) past the San Ignacio turnoff without seeing any evidence of a search. Based on my admittedly limited experience in Mexico, I was still fairly sure that there was a search party out looking. I just needed to find them. As the suspect had supposedly been from Coyotitán, I turned south and drove there. That town lies just a few miles off the main highway on the road leading to San Ignacio. I stopped at the gas station there to see if they might have seen any sign of the police, but the station was closed, and no one was around to question.

I was still fairly sure that if I kept looking, I would find them. I have always been accurately described as being persistent. I drove down the highway toward the site where the truck was supposedly abandoned, thinking they might be in that area by now. At this point around the 48-kilometer marker, something caught my eye. Near a white building and a turnoff for a microwave communications tower, I could just make out some activity down a dirt road. It could have just been some ranchers or farmers working, but I decided to drive down this dirt track and see what was happening. Even if it were only ranchers, they might have seen the police search party.

As I rounded a corner, ahead of me was a large, old battered white pickup surrounded by seven heavily-armed men and a man in handcuffs. The armed men were not in uniform. Rather, they were wearing old clothing including heavily worn and frankly mainly T-shirts full of holes. They had a collection of shotguns, rifles, and automatic weapons. In a normal situation, if I had encountered such a group on an isolated rural dirt road, I would have quickly turned the car around and driven away as fast as I could. But in this case, I said to myself, "Oh good, I have found the police!"

I got out of my car and walked over to the men and introduced myself. They were led by a man who identified himself as Lieutenant Guadalupe Leyva of the Culiacán Municipal Police. Culiacán, the state capital, lies roughly 100 miles north of where we were standing, and they were clearly outside of their normal jurisdiction. Lieutenant Leyva said the police were acting under the direct instructions of Sinaloa Governor Antonio Toledo Corro. He added that they had been out all night searching at a variety of locations and he seemed quite angry in addition to being very tired and frustrated.

The handcuffed man appeared to be roughly 15 to 18

years old, with long dark dirty hair. He was quite slender, almost emaciated, and about 5 feet, 11 inches tall. The police said his nickname was "El Pájaro" because people thought he looked like a bird. The suspect and another older man were apparently being sought in connection with the murder of Professor Schrock. The older man was identified by the police as Maclovio Lamarque Perrida, known as "El Nene" or "The Baby." He was 25 years old and had apparently been recently released from the Islas Marias prison that lies off the coast of Puerto Vallarta, where he had served time for some drug-related offenses. The policeman added that both men had been working at the gas station in Coyotitán.

At this point the narrative became a bit confused. Lieutenant Leyva said that Professor Schrock had stopped in Coyotitán, some distance off the main road, to buy his last 35 liters of gas. There, one of the suspects hitched a ride with Schrock and took him to where we now were, about 17 kilometers south of Coyotitán, where the two men stabbed Schrock to death, buried him and then drove the truck to where it was found abandoned. They would have driven the truck further, he added, but neither of the men knew how to drive well, so they just left it. He couldn't explain how the second man got to the site where the Professor was allegedly murdered or where they got a shovel to bury the body. There was nothing to indicate that Professor Schrock had brought a shovel with him to Mexico.

The police then led the youth to a nearby creek bed and requested the youth show them the exact spot where the body was buried. They uncuffed the suspect and gave him the shovel and told him to dig. The youth had apparently led the police to a number of different sites and a distance from each other during the night, all without success. For the next hour or so, we proceeded to several nearby areas where, at each one, the youth identified the spot but dug to no avail. The police were growing more and more angry and proceeded to begin using what some now refer to as "enhanced interrogation techniques", including direct physical abuse of the suspect. During this enhanced interrogation, the suspect continued to respond, "No sé nada" ("I don't know anything") as he fell. I asked the Lieutenant to stop abusing the suspect as it was both wrong and apparently ineffective. He responded that "this was his country, and the police would do what they felt like." After several further attempts to get them to stop, I repeated that his methods were not effective; I could not be a party to mistreatment; and I was heading back to Mazatlán to report in. Being in an isolated area surrounded by angry policemen, I couldn't think of anything else to do. It was also clear that it was unlikely that this search group would have any success that day.

In any event, the lieutenant said they would continue interrogating the suspect and others in the area and would continue to search for the body. They would keep the Consulate apprised of their progress. By now it was a little bit before 10 a.m. and so I returned to the main highway and drove south back to Mazatlán. I did not see any other police activity on the drive home.

At this point it seemed unclear to me whether the police had the right suspect and I reported so back to Washington and the Embassy. The police said the suspect admitted to knowing several things about the crime that only the murderer would know, such as that Professor Schrock had lots of wine with him. They also said he told them the crime took place around 4:00 p.m., which fit a plausible scenario regarding his travel plans. Finally, I questioned why the governor would have called the Consulate if the police were not fairly certain they had the right suspect. Still, the fact that the police had discovered no new physical evidence was disturbing, and the fact that they were resorting to torture was even worse.

During the day Acting Principal Officer Kramer met the various flights bringing Mrs. Schrock, Dr. Geer, and another relative of Mrs. Schrock and then escorted them to their hotel. This took a good portion of the day. Mrs. Schrock told us that she had been apprehensive about traveling to Mexico and in meeting with U.S. Consular and Mexican officials but felt better after being met by Consulate representatives when she arrived. During her visit and thereafter, although she and her party expressed extreme dissatisfaction with the lack of progress in finding her missing husband, they were always courteous with us and treated us well. If I had been in her situation, I am not sure I would have been as gracious.

We spent quite a bit of time briefing the party and going over the various facts as we knew them. She had a look at the truck and her husband's possessions in case they might spur a thought on a search avenue we had neglected. We also discussed returning the truck to the United States but agreed we should wait some weeks to pursue that issue. After this, we planned the next day's operations. Acting Principal Officer Kramer and Vice Consul Oreste would accompany Mrs. Schrock and Dr. Geer to the site where the truck was allegedly found by the police and then proceed to San Ignacio to talk with the mayor and city police. Two more of her relatives were arriving the next afternoon and we arranged to meet them. I would stay in Mazatlán and continue to follow up with the Mexican authorities by telephone, and frankly, to get some rest.

SUNDAY, JULY 4 - ELECTION DAY

The Fourth of July is an important day for diplomatic and consular offices throughout the world. It is normally marked with a formal reception of some sort and maybe a private event. This was not to be for Mazatlán. The press of business had not allowed time for planning for such an event, and, in reflection, it probably would have been inappropriate to host one. We did, however, manage to host a brief private gathering for consular staff and their families that afternoon at the empty consul's residence that focused on activities, including a piñata, for the children.

July Fourth was also election day in Mexico. When I called the Culiacán police chief that morning to see if they had made any further progress in searching for Professor Schrock's body, he responded negatively. He also said that the Culiacán police had suspended their search efforts as they were needed to provide security for election sites. The Mexican army was similarly engaged. He added, moreover, that his role in the case would be substantially reduced as the matter had been handed over to the Office of the Procuraduria General for Sinaloa which also had taken custody of the suspect, "El Pájaro." They still had not yet apprehended the second suspect, "El Nene." Mexico, like the United States, has a wide variety of law enforcement agencies. The Office of the Procuraduria General was just as the name translated into English stated, "Attorney General" and had broad law enforcement powers throughout the state of Sinaloa. We had dealt with the office previously and I knew the current director of the office, or attorney general, Jorge Chavez Castro. Calls to his office on a Sunday were, not surprisingly, unanswered. For better or worse, we were going to be in frequent contact with him and his office in the coming months.

The day's activities actually began much earlier. At 5:30 a.m., just as the sun was rising over the Pacific, Acting Principal Officer Kramer and Vice Consul Oreste picked up Mrs. Schrock, Dr. Geer and another family member at their hotel and then proceeded north to visit the various sites connected with Professor Schrock's disappearance. The group first walked the area where the truck had been discovered and then proceeded to the area near the microwave tower and white building where the Culiacán police had been searching for a body the day before. After visiting the gas station in Coyotitán where the arrested murder suspects had previously worked, they headed toward San Ignacio.

When the group reached that city, the police and Mexican army were fully occupied with providing security for polling places. They were able to talk briefly with the lieutenant in charge of the army detachment and the mayor of the city. Both independently said roughly the same thing: the Mexican government at all levels was continuing the investigation; a suspect had been arrested and was in custody in Culiacán, although he was denying any knowledge of the crime; and finally, that the other suspect was thought to have fled over the mountains to the neighboring state of Durango.

As one can imagine, the Schrock party was not at all heartened by any of this, or frankly, the very limited time the officials would spend with them. The party pressed the police chief on whether the suspect in custody was guilty since many people confess compulsively to things they had not done. (I had not mentioned the torture of "El Pájaro" to Mrs. Schrock or any of the family.) The police chief responded that Mexican authorities remained convinced that the young man they had arrested was the guilty party. From their remarks in the car on the drive back to Mazatlán, our consular officers said it seemed that the Schrock family did not share the police chief's confidence that they had arrested the right person. They were appreciative of the Consulate's assistance and said the visit to the various sites gave them a clearer frame of reference for understanding what they had been told about the various events.

Dr. Geer later reportedly told *The Arizona Republic* (July 14, 1982) that after his trip to San Ignacio, "he had doubted for more than a week that the youth ("El Pájaro") was the killer." The article continued quoting him as saying, "After I had been down there, I had been convinced that the San Ignacio people had not told everything they knew. It (the case) just didn't jibe with the usual modus operandi of the Mexican thieves," said Geer, who has lived in Mexico for brief periods over the past several years."

After they returned to Mazatlán, Acting Principal Officer Kramer drove Dr. Geer to the airport for his 12:30 p.m. flight back to Arizona. The two discussed the case and possible next steps and Dr. Geer said he would do whatever he could to help in the future. He had already done quite a bit. We had been in direct contact with him frequently via our telex system and he had always been responsive to our questions. He supplied such information as the Professor's eyeglass prescription and passport data quite early in the process when we needed information to assist in the search.

Kramer then waited at the airport to meet the arrival of two more relatives of Mrs. Schrock. When they arrived the atmosphere of the discussions shifted a bit. One of them suggested that the group, accompanied by Vice Consul Oreste, drive up to Culiacán in what the individual admitted was a long shot. He felt a face-to-face encounter with Mrs. Schrock might make the suspect confess. While I was not present for the discussion, I was later told that both Kramer and Oreste cast doubt on the proposal. They felt privately that they didn't want to put Mrs. Schrock through that ordeal and that it had very little, if any, chance of success. At the same time, it was already very late in the day and the long drive to Culiacán would have put them on a very hazardous highway long after dark, something contrary to Embassy travel guidelines and something we seldom did unless it was an emergency where a U.S. citizen needed immediate assistance. We did not want to put Mrs. Schrock and her family in unnecessary danger. The family finally agreed not to drive to Culiacán.

In response to our request for assistance with the media, the Embassy in Mexico City agreed to send us one of their experienced press officers for a short time. That officer, Tom Johnson, arrived in the afternoon and joined in with some of the discussions with Mrs. Schrock and our other visitors. He was quite helpful over the next few days.

The search for Professor Schrock took place at a

time when Mexico was experiencing major political changes and a rapidly deteriorating economic environment. As for the election, PRI candidate Miguel de la Madrid won with over 74 percent of the total vote (80 percent in Sinaloa). Although the elections are held in July, the president-elect does not take office until the following December 1st. The PRI also won 63 of the 64 seats in the Senate and 299 of the 400 seats in the lower chamber. The election took place in the midst of a serious and worsening economic crisis. With the collapse of oil prices in June 1981, Mexico lost a large portion of its export earnings and its federal revenues. In August of 1982, shortly after the election, the government declared a moratorium on its debt repayment which led to the rapid decline in the value of the peso and accelerating inflation.

On Monday, July 5, I drove Mrs. Schrock to the airport mid-morning for her return flight to Colorado. I ensured that she had all of our home and office telephone numbers and said that she should feel free to call us at all hours if she had any questions or information. I added that we would continue to actively search for her husband. Before she left, we again thoroughly reviewed her husband's possession and I transferred to her a brown nylon suitcase as well as all of the personal papers, including the ten unused American Express Travelers checks. We discussed the testing of the stains found in the truck and logistics regarding its eventual return. She also said she thought it would be useful to expand the radio and newspaper ads, perhaps with a reward for information leading to the discovery of her husband. Two of her relatives decided to stay in Mazatlán for a few more days although we had only infrequent contact with them during that time.

That same morning Vice Consul Oreste and the press officer from the Embassy in Mexico City accompanied members of the U.S. press to San Ignacio. The group spoke with the mayor and police chief but learned little new. The police chief added that he had little direct knowledge of the current investigation in Culiacán, since he was at the center point of the investigation and in daily contact with the attorney general's office. This trip led to a growing number of stories in the U.S. press regarding the missing Professor, although the finding of the truck on June 28 had already sharply increased interest and coverage in both the Mexican and U.S. press.

For some time, the Consulates, Embassy and Washington agencies had been working to collect any medical records or other information that might assist in the identification of a body if it turned out that the missing professor had been killed and his remains were recovered. Mrs. Schrock had brought Professor Schrock's dental records with her when she visited Mazatlán, but she decided to take them back with her when she left. Officials at the Embassy had reached out to the Department of Defense to see if they had any records concerning service by Professor Schrock. During July, the Embassy received several responses to these requests. Apparently, Professor Schrock had served in the Ohio National Guard from April 1957 through January 1960. He then joined the U.S. Air Force in 1961 and was honorably discharged in 1963. (He had also been honorably discharged from the National Guard.) Unfortunately, the information was extremely sketchy as his personnel files had been destroyed in a July 1973 fire at an Overland, Missouri storage facility. All the information the Air Force had was on papers akin to index cards. Thus, no additional material was available from his service records to aid in identification.

TUESDAY, JULY 6 - THE RAINS BEGIN

The next few days were relatively uneventful. We did not realize at the time that it was the calm before the storm, but we should have. Consulate officials in Mexico City, Mazatlán, Guadalajara and Hermosillo continued to push law enforcement in Mexico to make stronger efforts in their search for Professor Schrock. In Mazatlán we also tried in vain to find out more regarding the investigation of "El Pájaro" and "El Nene." Law enforcement officials in Sinaloa were extremely tight-lipped.

The State Department issued new press guidance at the noon press briefing on July 6, 1982, which read as follows:

Q: Has there been any further developments in the case of William (sic) Schrock, the American who disappeared in Mexico?

A: American Officials in Mazatlán continue to work closely with Mexican federal, state and local authorities in their efforts to locate Mr. Schrock. However, as of now the continuing investigations have not uncovered any information which would lead to Mr. Schrock's whereabouts or condition.

Q: Has there been an analysis of the stains found in Mr. Schrock's vehicle?

A: As we have previously mentioned, a substance

has been found in Mr. Schrock's vehicle. We understand that the vehicle contained only a small amount of the substance, and its nature has not yet been determined. However, efforts to identify its contents are continuing.

Q: Have any suspects been picked up in connection with Mr. Schrock's disappearance?

A: We understand that police authorities in Culiacán, Mexico (about 125 miles north of Mazatlán) are questioning a suspect thought to be involved in a number of car robberies in the area. The suspect was arrested on June 9. Although he is being questioned on Mr. Schrock's disappearance, as far as we know there has been no connection established between the suspect and Mr. Schrock.

Regarding the stains found in Professor Schrock's truck, on July 6, the day after the departure of Mrs. Schrock, with her and the Embassy's concurrence, we carefully cut out several portions of the passenger seat upholstery and the flooring, sealed them in separate packages and sent them by special courier to the Embassy in Mexico City to forward for further action. The Embassy sent them to Washington agencies for a more thorough examination.

On July 7, the Department also sent us an additional series of questions from Mrs. Schrock. It noted that seventeen members of Congress were interested in the case but did not name them other than Senator Gary Hart of Colorado. The main question in this message was whether or not the jail in San Ignacio had ever been searched to determine if Mr. Schrock is or ever was there and whether other prisoners had been questioned. I think this was likely an old question from the previous week as I had personally briefed Mrs. Schrock when she was in Mazatlán of the detailed searches we undertook of the San Ignacio police compound on June 28 and 29. We subsequently again detailed the Consulate's search of the San Ignacio police complex and jail in a message sent early Monday, July 12.

Our efforts over the next weeks were to be further hampered by the onset of the rainy season in Sinaloa. On the evening of Thursday, June 8, the first rains began in the Mazatlán area. The rainy season normally begins around July 1 and continues through October. It is characterized by extremely heavy rains and large, powerful thunderstorms. Evidence may be washed away or buried if located in low-lying areas or in steam beds. It also causes flooding on city roads and local highways making driving even more hazardous. The intensity of the rains on the evening of June 8 indicated that we were in for a very wet season.

FRIDAY, JULY 9 - THE REWARD

By now a month had passed since the Consulate in Mazatlán had been notified of the disappearance of Professor Schrock and almost six weeks since his entry in Mexico. Although we had found his pickup truck and many of his possessions, his whereabouts remained a mystery. The Mexican law enforcement agencies were not as forthcoming with us as they might have been regarding any progress they were making. To further complicate things, on Friday, July 9 Agustin Jaime Lopez Montoya, the Director Gobernación for the state of Sinaloa and his deputy Fausto Medina "resigned" from their positions. Although I hadn't mentioned in this narrative much of my communication with them over the past few weeks, these two individuals had been quite forthcoming in the search for Professor Schrock and were important contacts for helping to discern what claims were true and what were false. At the time I wondered if their departure was due to their cooperation with the Consulate during the search for Professor Schrock or was related to some other internal struggle within the Sinoloan government. One of them later told me they were both forced out of office. In any event, their resignations were to remove a valuable source for the Consulate of accurate information on what was actually happening within the Sinaloa government in the coming days when we really needed one.

That same day agents from the Federal Tourism Ministry appeared at the Consulate in Mazatlán to offer their assistance. They said they were there at the request of the cabinet-level head of Federal Tourism, Rosa Luz Alegria. This was at least some evidence that interest in the case was continuing at senior levels in Mexico. After a thorough briefing by Consulate staff, the officials promised to provide assistance with the search for Professor Schrock. During the coming months they actually did provide us with some useful information on what was happening in Mexico City, although it was of little use in finding the Professor.

As I noted previously, we had been in discussion with Mrs. Schrock, Dr. Geer and others regarding possible ways to expand the search efforts. On July 9, officials from the University of Colorado Foundation notified the State Department's Citizens Emergency Center that they wished to offer a $5,000 reward for positive information leading to the discovery of the whereabouts of Professor Schrock. The University of Colorado Foundation is a private corporation that manages funds to be used for university purposes.

The head of the Citizen's Emergency Center called me to discuss how the Consulate might publicize the reward and then sent us instructions outlining the details along with a draft announcement in English. Information-only copies of this message were also sent to the Embassy in Mexico City and to the Consulates in Hermosillo and Guadalajara. The idea would be for Mazatlán's consular staff to select three-to-five newspapers, based on our judgment of their coverage area, and to run two-to-three ads in each publication for a week. Based on our reporting of the response to the announcement, the University of Colorado Foundation, which would pay for ads, would then decide whether to continue or expand them. We were also given discretion to translate the reward amount into Mexican pesos in the announcement, but we felt a dollar reward would catch more attention. The instructions emphasized two additional aspects. First, the message had to be clear that the reward would only be paid if the information provided proved to be accurate and led to the location of Professor Schrock. Second, it should be made clear that this was a private, not a U.S. government, reward offer, and the Consulate was only assisting with the administrative arrangements.

The Department sent a separate message to Mexico City on July 9 on another matter. It noted that Mrs. Schrock acknowledged that consular officers are not trained investigators, and that was not their role. She, therefore, suggested instead that the Embassy assign someone to search for Professor Schrock who: a) is an American; b) reports to the Ambassador; c) is not a diplomat but rather an experienced professional investigator; d) would not usurp the Mexican authorities but could make suggestions on how they should proceed; and e) have the clout to push for results. The person would need to be familiar with the country and speak fluent Spanish. The U.S. official Mrs. Schrock spoke with in Washington indicated that the Foreign Service does not employ such a "category" of person but agreed to pass the suggestion on to the Embassy and other posts in Mexico. Mrs. Schrock added that she had already engaged a private investigator through a lawyer in Hermosillo. That investigator later came by the Consulate in Mazatlán but did not develop any useful information during the search for Professor Schrock, nor did he seem particularly knowledgeable about western Mexico.

On the following Tuesday Ambassador John Gavin sent a cable to Washington (with a short message to be passed on to Mrs. Schrock). It read:

> Dear Mrs. Schrock:
> I refer to your request that I assign a professional investigator to search for your husband, Nicholas W. Schrock.
>
> I regret that the person you specified in your telex to me and in your conversation with an officer of the Department of State does not exist on my staff.
>
> The primary responsibility for the continued search for your husband and clarification of the circumstances of his disappearance belongs to the appropriate Mexican law enforcement authorities. The role of the government of the United States in general, and of the Embassy and United States consular officers in Mexico specifically, is to do all possible to assure that the Mexicans comply with their responsibilities. This we have done, are doing, and will continue to do.
>
> John Gavin
> Ambassador
> Embassy Mexico City, Mexico

The instructions from Washington regarding the media and reward campaign meant it was to be another working weekend in Mazatlán. We had hoped it might be a bit quieter. We were lucky that our telex machine was operating that day. It had continued to break down sporadically over the past couple of weeks making communications more complicated. We spent a good portion of the day translating the English text of the reward into suitable Spanish and contacting newspapers in Sinaloa regarding placing the ads. We telegraphed to Washington that beginning July 10 (that Saturday) ads would begin appearing for free in the *Noroeste de Mazatlán*. On Sunday, July 11, additional paid ads would be placed in the *Sol Del Pacifico* of Mazatlán, and we intended to place ads in several other newspapers in Los Mochis, Culiacán and Mazatlán as early as Monday, July 13. Fairly fast work for a weekend. We also included the text of the reward offer in Spanish for the Embassy's and Department's review and suggested that all ads also contain a large photo of Professor Schrock. The text of the ad was short, announcing the reward and providing a physical description of the Professor and his travel plans. Our outgoing cable also noted that none of these or previous expenditures on announcements would be charged to Mrs. Schrock; rather we would, at their request, bill officials at the University of Colorado Foundation. Washington also very helpfully cabled us the legal and financial authority to expend up to $300 for the advertisements, which the Foundation had sent by Western Union to the Department.

We included in the above cable a note to the Consulate in Hermosillo indicating DFS agents from Sonora continued to appear at Consulate Mazatlán requesting briefings on the Schrock disappearance. A group that arrived that Saturday said they were currently using helicopters to try to locate one or more suspects in the Durango area. Neither our Consulate nor the Consulate in Hermosillo was ever able to verify the use by Mexican authorities of helicopters in the search. We also apologized to Hermosillo for not responding to some of their messages more quickly as our telex had been out of operation at various times over the past couple of weeks and we had not received their initial updates and questions.

In addition, on Saturday, July 10, while we were in the middle of preparing an extensive ad campaign, the Consulate in Mazatlán bade farewell to Acting Principal Officer Ron Kramer and his family. They were driving back to Monterrey, Mexico where Kramer worked at the Consulate General. He had been a welcome and essential part of the team during his time in Mazatlán and would be missed in the coming days. From the moment he arrived, he showed he was well-organized and a tireless worker. He also volunteered to do most of the more onerous routine consular matters, such as adjudicating non-immigrant visas, freeing up Vice Consul Oreste and I to focus more on the search for Professor Schrock and other pressing consular emergencies.

SUNDAY, JULY 11 - THE BODY FOUND?

Vice Consul Oreste and I took Sunday morning off. We and our staff had spent part of the previous few days ensuring that the consul's residence and office were in good shape. In midafternoon, the new Principal Officer, Elayne Urban, drove into town and met us at the residence where we began her orientation and helped her get settled. She was an experienced consular officer and was, she said, "ready to get to work!" We agreed to meet later that afternoon at the Consulate where we briefed the new principal officer on the Professor Schrock case as well as on other matters and planned our operations and her orientation for the next few days. A good portion of an officer's initial time at a new assignment is spent making calls on different contacts and officials and getting a better understanding of the local politics and problems. We bade her a good night and headed home.

We had thought this might be a somewhat quiet weekend, but we were totally wrong. This was to be a challenging introduction to Sinaloa for our new principal officer. Consular officers in Mazatlán, like other posts, had developed an extensive and effective web of contacts throughout our consular district over the years. While one always had to be careful in listening to them as they often had their own agenda or political ax to grind in talking to us, they did provide useful information.

About 8:15 in the evening Jose Rico Mendiola, mayor of Mazatlán, called Vice Consul Oreste to say that Sinoloan state authorities had discovered the body of Professor Schrock near San Ignacio, but he had little additional information. (The mayor was a good friend of Oreste and often called him to discuss interesting local developments.) Oreste then called Elayne Urban and me at our respective homes to report what he had heard. I immediately called the Office of the Procuraduria General in Culiacán as that agency now had lead jurisdiction for the Sinoloan government in the search for Professor Schrock. Using after-hours telephone numbers provided for use with this case, I tried to reach Jorge Chavez Castro, the director of the Procuraduria General (the state attorney general). I was able to reach some of his staff and eventually his secretary, Mercedes Salazar. They had little additional information, but Salazar confirmed that a body had been found but had not yet arrived in Culiacán and was being sent to the San Martin Funeral Home in that city. They "believed" it to be the body of Professor Schrock. She also said she did not know why her agency had not called us with this information.

Shortly thereafter we received a call from Raul Arho, an agent for the federal DFS, who independently verified the information we had from Mazatlán's mayor and from Culiacán. He added that the body was found through the questioning of "different suspects" than those questioned before ("El Pájaro" and "El Nene"). He asked that the press not be notified as that might interfere with the ongoing investigation because some suspects were not in custody. After comparing notes among ourselves in Mazatlán, we called the Operations Center in Washington, D.C., and the consular duty officer at the Embassy in Mexico City to report what we had heard and prepared for a long week of work. Given our previous experience in this case with the premature announcement of the discovery of a body, we decided to hold off making additional calls to the United States until we had a chance to further verify what was actually happening.

At 7:15 a.m., Mexico DFS agent Arho again called consular officials in Mazatlán. He repeated the information provided the previous evening but had no new information. He said he was mainly calling to maintain contact with us and again to strongly urge that the press not be notified regarding the finding of the body as they were still searching for some of the suspects.

After repeated efforts, at about 8:15 a.m., I was able to reach state Attorney General Jorge Chavez Castro at his office in Culiacán. He seemed somewhat surprised by our call, although I and other officials had talked to him previously about the Schrock case and other matters. He confirmed that a body had been found and was now in Culiacán. Chavez Castro added that it was in such a state of decomposition that they would need dental records or someone who knew Professor Schrock well to positively identify the body. Given the state of decomposition, he doubted that fingerprints could be used for identification. He said the body had an injury or defect in the right leg, apparently from well before his disappearance. We had not heard of any such problems or previous injury to Professor Schrock's leg but said we would see what we could find out. Despite repeated questioning as to where the body had been found, Chavez Castro would only say "in the area around San Ignacio," which to me included the location where the truck was found.

The state Attorney General then added that the body had been found with a Casio watch with a black band. Mrs. Schrock had earlier told us that the missing watch was a Timex. There had also been a ring that apparently had been removed and sold to a third party. He also mentioned a pair of half glasses for reading found with the body. We agreed to talk again later that day.

Consular officers then called Larry Lane, the recently-arrived consul general in Mexico City who supervised all U.S. consular activities in Mexico and briefed him on the evening's and morning's events. It was then about 8:40 in the morning. He said he would call Mrs. Schrock to let her know the current developments and would also try to secure copies of the dental records. We also discussed sending a consular officer to Culiacán to try to view the body, but Lane indicated it would be best to wait until we had some clarity on when we might have dental records or other materials to help identify Professor Schrock. As we were not investigators, we were also not forensic pathologists and thus our presence in Culiacán would have been of limited use in helping to identify a reportedly severely decomposed body. We continued to work the phones and our network of contacts to try to gain additional information. We also sent a cable to Washington and the relevant parties in Mexico outlining what we had learned. We always followed up with a reporting cable even after calling in to Washington or the Embassy as the cable was more broadly circulated and thus reached more of those involved.

Principal Office Urban also decided that the Consulate

staff would continue its efforts, already underway, to place a series of ads in various newspapers in Sinaloa just in case the unidentified body that was reportedly recovered turned out not to be that of Professor Schrock. At this time, it was not as if we had any doubts regarding the identity, but the senior Sinaloa state law enforcement official had only said they believed they had found the Professor's body and were trying to identify it. These efforts to place ads would continue throughout the week, as previously requested by the University of Colorado Foundation.

As the day wore on, we were in frequent direct contact with Mrs. Schrock and with Dr. Geer. Mrs. Schrock, with minor assistance from the Consulate, was able to arrange to have Professor Schrock's dental records hand-carried from Colorado to Mazatlán later that same day by personnel of Mexicana Airlines. Vice Consul Oreste met the Mexicana flight and immediately dispatched the records to the attorney general's office in Culiacán using a special courier provided by Mazatlán Mayor Rico. Mrs. Schrock also provided us, first over the telephone and then in writing, a written description of the dental records and a description of Professor Schrock's scars and other physical characteristics that we translated into Spanish and forwarded to Culiacán.

About 8:40 p.m., I called state Attorney General Chavez Castro to see if the dental records had been delivered and whether he could provide any other information regarding the progress on the case. He thanked the Consulate for the quick response and confirmed his office had received the records and provided them to his forensic team. He resisted repeated requests for more information regarding possible suspects and the investigation. I also pressed him as to where the body had been recovered. After a long pause he said cryptically that "it had been found buried in the (main) cemetery in San Ignacio." That information not only surprised me, but also sent a chill down my spine. It implied some degree of involvement by the San Ignacio police, a thought which I believed was a possibility and now which seemed more likely. I pressed for more details, but that was all he would say, so we agreed to talk again in the morning. I telephoned Principal Officer Consul Urban, the consular duty officer in Mexico City, the Operations Center in Washington, D.C. and Mrs. Schrock to tell them the records had arrived in Culiacán. With Mrs. Schrock, I emphasized again that the Mexican officials so far only believed they had found a body, but hopefully, we would have some clarity soon.

TUESDAY, JULY 13 - THE BODY IDENTIFIED?

Part of the consular staff's normal morning routine was to scan copies of the major newspapers in Mazatlán and the rest of Sinaloa and Nayarit for reports on developments that might affect consular operations, such as the arrest of a U.S. citizen, or that might affect U.S. relations with Mexico. We often got important and early tips from the papers that allowed us to respond quickly to help U.S. citizens. The local university student groups would advertise in the papers on the days they planned to demonstrate at the Consulate so that we could take additional steps to secure the entrances to the Consulate and buy materials to paint over the inevitable graffiti left on the outside of the building and the neighboring residences. That was quite helpful and much appreciated.

On the morning of Tuesday, July 13, at about 7:30 a.m., we read in the newspaper *Noroeste de Culiacán* a report that the body of Professor Schrock had been found strangled and half-buried in a grave near San Ignacio. The short article said four police officers from San Ignacio, including the police chief, had been in custody for 15 days. (Vice Consul Oreste had spoken personally with the police chief on July 5 while accompanying members of the U.S. press to San Ignacio, so that portion of the story seemed wrong.)

At about 8:10 a.m., I reached Mercedes Salazar, secretary

to the Sinoloan Attorney General Chavez Castro, and she verified the general contents of the *Noroeste* article, but noted the body was found fully buried in the cemetery and that the cause of death had not been established. She also confirmed that the San Ignacio police chief was among the five or six suspects in custody. I asked her to please have the attorney general call us with an update when he had a moment. We reported this information to Mexico City and Washington by cable and continued to gather further information.

At 10:15 a.m. State Attorney General Jorge Chavez Castro called the Consulate in Mazatlán to tell us that the body had been positively identified through dental checks, blood type and through the description of physical characteristics forwarded by Mazatlán. He said that there were six policemen and one civilian in custody. The mayor of San Ignacio was not being held. Three suspects were arrested for robbery and murder and the other four for assisting in the disposal of the body. Chavez Castro said Professor Schrock was killed when he resisted a personal search that was part of the robbery. He said the cause of death was choking, probably due to a blow to the neck. The body, he said, was buried near the scene of the crime and then reburied in the cemetery in San Ignacio. The police chief was only being held for knowledge of the reburial. The Consulate then notified the State Department's Office of Citizen Services and the Embassy in Mexico City of the positive identification. Before he hung up, Chavez Castro said he would be making an official statement within an hour. The press conference was extensively covered by the Mexican press and appeared in numerous U.S. and Mexican newspapers the following day.

His remarks followed closely what he had told us: Professor Schrock had been killed by members of the San Ignacio police and secretly buried in the cemetery in San Ignacio. Chavez Castro named seven individuals in police custody who would be charged for various crimes: Deputy Police Chief Arnulfo Velarde Cruz, Police Chief Roberto Velazquez Treviño, Ismael Garcia Olivas, David Antonio Valenzuela Osuna, Ignacio Zuñiga Aguilar, Lazaro Martinez Ontiveros and Valentin Murguia Quintero. He added that an eighth suspect, Claudio Lamarque Pereda or "El Nene" was being sought. Interestingly, the police had previously identified "El Nene" as Maclovio Lamarque Perrida.

Chavez Castro added that two of the suspects, police officers Ismael Garcia Olivas and Daniel Antonio Valenzuela Osuna, were found to be in possession of clothing identified as belonging to the missing professor. That might explain why we found relatively few items of clothing in the truck. However, that didn't necessarily mean they were guilty of the murder of the Professor. They could have been guilty looting an abandoned vehicle. Chavez Castro continued saying these two police officers had decided to confess and also named their accomplices who were then subsequently arrested.

In his press conference, the attorney general said he wanted to emphasize two additional points. First, the U.S. Federal Bureau of Investigation was not involved in the capture or questioning of the suspects. (He then named the various Mexican law enforcement agencies, as well as the Mexican army, that had been involved in the process.) The attorney general also said he wanted to categorically deny that San Ignacio Mayor Francisco Javier Palacios had any knowledge of, or participation in, the crimes. Some of the initial articles in the Mexican press had implied the mayor was involved or reported he had been arrested. Finally, Chavez Castro said the body would be transferred to the American Consulate in Mazatlán. That was one aspect that he had not discussed with us over the phone.

This news, of course, sparked intensive press coverage over the next few days and was covered extensively by the *Noroeste* of Mazatlán in a July 14 article. Other articles supplemented this one with additional details. On July 15, the Mexico City-based English language newspaper, *The Nation*, quoted extensively from comments attributed to Juan Ramon Martinez Arbon, a spokesman for the attorney general's office. According to the spokesman, the San Ignacio police chief and two accomplices allegedly saw Professor Schrock pay cash at a local gas station and intercepted the truck further down the road to rob him.

This was a slight variation on the police charges against "El Pájaro" and "El Nene" albeit with direct police participation. Articles in the *El Sol del Pacifico* and *Excelsior of Mexico City* printed that the deputy police chief participated in the killing, but shortly thereafter told the police chief. The *Excelsior* article also noted that the mayor had authorized the San Ignacio police to use the Professor's truck to support the PRI efforts in the federal election campaign, something I had witnessed June 28.

The Nation's July 15 account also reported that the attorney general's spokesman, Martinez Arbon, said that Professor Schrock's body was first buried in a ravine about 100 yards from where he was murdered and later reburied in the main cemetery in San Ignacio. The breakthrough, he added, occurred when an investigator noticed one of the policemen wearing "American-made clothes." This sounded odd to me at the time as many Mexican citizens in that part of the country were making shopping trips to the United States, or otherwise wearing "American-made clothes" such as jeans.

The Nation's article ended by saying that Professor Schrock's body had been turned over to the custody of the U.S. Consulate in Mazatlán and will be shipped to Colorado for burial. (This last statement was not true as the Consulate almost never took custody of a body but only facilitated its transfer.)

With a large number of persons traveling and living on both sides of the border and having relatives on both sides, the normal transfer of a body, while somewhat bureaucratic, was a relatively straightforward process. It could, understandably, be done in a fairly expeditious manner over a couple of days. For a body to be shipped to the United States, the Mexican government would need to produce a death certificate and other paperwork that was essentially permission to transfer the body along with forms addressing health department concerns.

In the case of a U.S. citizen, the Consulate would issue a "Report of Death of an American Citizen Abroad" and help either the funeral home or the family – or both – to satisfy U.S. Customs and other requirements. It was not a difficult process. The body itself would normally be prepared for shipment by a funeral home in Mexico and then transferred directly to the transportation company shipping the remains to the United States. The shipping company would then, after clearing routine U.S. entry procedures, deliver the remains directly to agents of a funeral home in the United States. That was the normal process.

So shortly after the mid-morning notification by the state attorney general of the positive identification and before the press conference, Mrs. Schrock and Dr. Geer – among others – were notified of the identification. We also confirmed directly with Mrs. Schrock that her wish was that the remains be transferred as soon as possible to Boulder, Colorado, where she lived. We told her we would let her know as soon as the arrangements were set up. Officials from both the University of Colorado and Thunderbird said they would be ready and able to assist in the transfer if necessary and were quite helpful.

We also called Jose Borboa, manager of the funeral home "San Martin" in Culiacán, since the attorney general's office had told us he had the body. While Mr. Borboa was actually somewhat vague regarding whether his establishment actually had the remains at the time, he did confirm his funeral home would be transferring it and working on the necessary paperwork. We made sure he had all of our contact telephone numbers and told him to call us at all hours if he needed assistance.

A next step for the Consulate would be to prepare the "Report of Death of an American Citizen Abroad", but for that we needed a death certificate issued by the local authorities. Despite repeated calls to various Mexican state offices in Culiacán, we were unable to get any further information, nor a good idea of when the death certificate would be forthcoming. In almost all of the other death cases we had worked on in the last six months, the local authorities had been relatively expeditious in providing the necessary documents.

WEDNESDAY, JULY 14 - DELAYS AND DOUBTS

At some point on the afternoon of July 13 or July 14, officials from the University of Colorado confirmed the name and address of the U.S. funeral home in Boulder that would receive the expatriated remains. Those officials also said the university would be paying for transportation costs and were briefed on how to make the transfer of funding. That formal authorization to pay the Mexican funeral and transportation costs was received July 16 by Consulate Mazatlán, which would then handle the payments. We had received verbal authorization from the Department on the morning of July 15.

Arrangements were also made with Mexicana Airlines, which would ship the body from Mazatlán to Denver. Mexicana's staff said that due to heavy demand for shipping air freight, the airline would not be able to transport the remains until the afternoon of July 15.

As in many matters that draw the public's attention, this one was consistently surrounded by wild rumors. That day, Wednesday, July 14, articles began appearing in the local newspapers stating that the death of Professor Schrock was not an isolated event. The reports said that other Americans had been murdered and buried in the San Ignacio graveyard. These reports of other murders in San Ignacio came up from time-to-time over the following weeks. We carefully checked for any reports of other U.S. citizens that might be missing in the area and didn't find any evidence of other disappearances. We also followed up with Mexican authorities directly on this matter and never found anything to indicate they were anything more than rumors, although there was evidence the Mexican authorities were later digging in the San Ignacio cemetery to see if they might discover other victims. There were also press rumors the following day that the mayor of San Ignacio was also being held in the death of Professor Schrock.

That afternoon the Consulate received a letter addressed to Consul Urban from Jorge Chavez Castro, Attorney General for the state of Sinaloa, expressing his and his state's sincere condolences for the death of Professor Schrock to the Consulate and the family of the Professor. It is interesting that although we were able to get a letter of condolences that quickly, we still did not have a death certificate.

By now it was late on the afternoon of July 14, and we still did not have the Mexican death certificate and other papers necessary to ship the body. This was more than 24 hours after the announcement of the positive identification, and it was unusual for the issuance of a death certificate to take so long, particularly in such a high-profile case. Calls to the funeral home only confirmed that they had the body and it was ready for shipment, but their staff denied any knowledge of the status of the necessary documents. Calls to the attorney general's office and other contacts within the state government were also unsuccessful. The attorney general's office was particularly evasive. We sent a cable to Washington and the relevant U.S. diplomatic and consular posts in Mexico that read in part:

Death certificate has not been transmitted to Consulate as of 19:00 July 14, 1982, but is expected to arrive in time for the body to be shipped July 15, 1982, to Denver, Colorado. Until that time body is being held in San Martin Funeral Home in Culiacán, Sinaloa. Lack of flights to Colorado and delay in preparing of paperwork for shipment by Mexican officials caused delay in shipment.

Post is attempting to determine further details of the incident. Rumors in Mexican press of more AmCits (American citizens) buried in cemetery have not been verified and appear to be just rumors; However, post will press for further investigation to be sure no other AmCits were involved in similar events. Post will update.

THURSDAY, JULY 15 - A BODY SHIPPED

What should have been a routine transfer of the remains of an U.S. citizen back to the United States ended up being extremely chaotic. Early morning attempts to reach various state officials, including the attorney general who would not take our calls, did not provide us any additional information regarding developments in the case or the status of the necessary paperwork. We called Consul General Larry Lane in Mexico City to let him know there were unexplained delays, and we would keep him posted. While I don't have any documents to verify this, my memory of the event is that the relevant Mexicana flight was not scheduled to depart for Colorado until late afternoon. Calls to the funeral home indicated the body was still in Culiacán, more than 100 miles to the north, as they had not yet received instructions to move it. They said they were ready to proceed as soon as instructed and should be able to make the scheduled flight.

This delay made all of us at the Consulate, as well as those U.S. officials in Mexico City like Larry Lane, concerned that something might be seriously wrong with the body or its identification. Very few things involving this case were simple. At the same time the Schrock family and the officials at Thunderbird were pushing for a quick return of the body to the United States, we were beginning to have serious doubts.

Finally, late that morning or very early in the afternoon of the scheduled flight, a courier arrived with the Mexican death certificate and other necessary paperwork. At about the same time, the funeral home in Culiacán called to tell us that they had received their instructions from the attorney general's office and were proceeding to the Mazatlán airport. While they expected to arrive just under an hour before the flight was to leave, they had contacted Mexicana Airlines and they (the funeral home) thought they had enough time to handle the necessary formalities and still make the flight. We told them one of our vice consuls would meet them at the airport to provide any assistance necessary. We also confirmed directly with Mexicana airlines that they were expecting the remains and would do everything they could to ensure the transfer went well.

Even on a cursory reading, it was immediately apparent that there were numerous irregularities with the Mexican certificate of death. It did not give a date, location, or cause of death, but rather said:

En virtud del avanzado estado de descomposición del cadáver no se pudo determinar la causa directa y necesaria de la muerte. (Due to the advanced state of decomposition of the body the direct cause of death could not be determined.)

We began to prepare the "Report of Death of an American Citizen Abroad", a copy of which we would send with the body. This is a basic legal document recognized by courts and financial institutions in the United States in winding up a person's affairs after death. Still, due to the late arrival of the necessary papers from the Mexican officials, we were quickly running out of time to finalize that and other documents necessary for the shipment.

As I was preparing the draft Report, Esteban Guzman, one of our more experienced Mexican national employees (he had worked with us for more than twenty years), walked over to me and asked, "So how are you wording the Report?"

I immediately put my pen down (this was only the draft; we would finalize it using one of our aging IBM Selectric II typewriters) and paid attention. When Mr. Guzman suspected something was wrong, he often did not directly state so, but would begin asking questions. He had helped me on several occasions to avoid making a mistake, or by clarifying an issue, so I learned to always listen to him when he had questions. Clearly, he had concerns that something might be wrong.

"What do you mean?", I asked. The normal practice on these certificates was to rely on either the verification of the individual by Mexican authorities or by next-of-kin. The identity of the individual in the U.S. report would mirror the general details of the Mexican death certificate, supplementing them as needed. "Have you seen the body?" he asked. "No", I responded, although in most cases, particularly when the body is in an advanced state of decomposition, we don't view them, but relied again on the identification of family or Mexican officials. On several occasions, I had identified a body based on photos or with the assistance of a relative. In this case we only had a positive identification from the Mexican doctor who had signed the death certificate. Mr. Guzman then said, "Since you haven't seen the body, you might want to note on the Report that it is *"Nicholas Wickham Schrock as identified by Dr. ....",* which we did.

As soon as the paperwork was ready Vice Consul Oreste

headed for the airport to see if he could get there before the Mexicana flight departed. He arrived less than an hour before the departure, but just in time to assist with the flight. Shortly after his arrival, the hearse containing the remains drove up and was loaded onto the waiting plane. The body was being shipped un-embalmed to allow for a more thorough autopsy in the United States should the family wish it. Professor Schrock's passport, dental records and other materials, were loosely attached to the coffin by Mexicana Airline officials. Vice Consul Oreste waited until the flight took off and as it departed into the sunset, he drove back to the Consulate to report in. We then called the State Department in Washington, the Embassy in Mexico City and Mrs. Schrock to let them know the body had departed. We followed up with a reporting cable and turned to other matters.

FRIDAY, JULY 16 - DOUBTS CONFIRMED

Our chance of having a quiet Friday hadn't been very good in recent weeks, and this one was not to be an exception. It started out relatively slowly. We reviewed the local newspapers to see if they had any new information. Other than repeating rumors and previous developments, the articles added little to our knowledge. We made calls to various law enforcement officials to see if there were new developments and push them to continue to intensify their investigation.

We contacted Attorney General Chavez Castro and requested a written report on the investigation and suspects which he had promised to provide. He also said he would send along other physical property of the Professor from the San Ignacio police that his officials had recovered during the investigation. We again pressed for an explanation as to why we had not been notified of the discovery of the vehicle as we had a copy of a telegram dated June 9th addressed to an official of Gobernación in Culiacán reporting the discovery of the Professor's pickup. That delay had cost us three weeks when we would have had a better chance of finding out what happened to Professor Schrock. Chavez Castro deflected this issue but did deny reports we had received from the Mazatlán police that Mayor Palacios of San Ignacio was in custody. About the only other noteworthy item that day was the State

Department reported that, as of that date, there had been no further activity on Professor Schrock's credit card after he paid for his hotel in Hermosillo and that none of his traveler's checks had been cashed.

It turns out that our Consulate employee, Esteban Guzman, and others of us were right to be suspicious over the delay in providing a Mexican death certificate. Apparently just before 5 p.m. Washington D.C. time, Mrs. Schrock called Dr. Arnold Weber, President of the University of Colorado, and reported that the pathologists had completed an examination of the body shipped to Denver and had determined that it was definitely not Professor Schrock. Dr. Weber then called the State Department in Washington to outline his conversation with Mrs. Schrock and requested action by the U.S. government. It was not to be a quiet Friday night, nor a quiet weekend. Thoughtfully, the officer in the Department then immediately called the Consulate in Mazatlán to let us know what had transpired.

Then a series of rapid actions and telephone calls were made in both Sinaloa and the United States. The Consulate had had a previous case where the wrong body had been shipped from the United States to Mazatlán for burial. In that case one of two bodies recovered in a plane accident had been misidentified and sent to Mexico. We, therefore, decided the first thing to do was to check to ensure there had not been some mishandling along the way. Esteban Guzman, our experienced Mexican consular employee, had a long talk with the director of the funeral home in Culiacan and an employee that had accompanied the body to the airport. They were emphatic in saying the body they received from the attorney general's office was the one their employee had watched loaded onto the Mexicana flight. They added that there could not have been a mix-up at the funeral home in Culiacán as that was the only body that had been in the funeral home at that time.

Vice Consul Oreste spoke at length with an official at Mexicana Airlines, who then checked a few facts and called him back. The body transported by them from Mazatlán was the only one shipped from Mazatlán that day and was delivered directly to representatives of the funeral home in Colorado. In fact, it was the only body shipped by Mexicana Airlines either within Mexico or to the United States on July 15th.

While these calls were going on, I attempted to reach Attorney General Jorge Chavez Castro, although I doubted I would get through as we had had trouble reaching his office for the past couple of days. Surprisingly, with very little difficulty, I was able to speak directly to the attorney general, I quickly told him what had happened and asked for an explanation. I was astonished when he then blurted out in Spanish, "But you told me you were going to cremate the body!" First of all, I never said anything of the sort as it would be up to Mrs. Schrock. While she had mentioned cremation after positive identification when she visited Mazatlán and San Ignacio over the weekend of July Fourth, we had certainly never communicated her private conversations to the Mexican authorities. We also didn't get the impression that she had made a final decision regarding burial or cremation when we talked to her in the days leading up to the shipment of the body.

I took the attorney general's outburst as an implied admission that he had ordered the return of a body that he knew not to be Professor Schrock. That would explain the delay in the issuance of a Mexican death certificate. Perhaps they had gotten cold feet upon informing us for the second time that they had found Professor Schrock's body, when they in fact had not. The attorney general, of course, did not explicitly admit this and said that the body was really in a bad state of composition. I followed up by indicating that the Embassy would expect a full explanation and an energetic resumption of search efforts for Professor Schrock.

At the Consulate in Mazatlán, we also made calls to other Mexican law enforcement agencies, including DFS, and pressed them to resume their investigations and their search for Professor Schrock. We then called the Consul General in Mexico City, Larry Lane, and the Citizens Emergency Center in Washington to report on what we had learned. Given the sensitivity of the attorney general's remarks and the fact that some of our reporting cables had been passed to the news media, I did not include the remarks in my cables. I did tell Larry Lane in Mexico City and the Citizens Emergency Center on the telephone about the remarks and my conclusions.

After calling the Consulate in Mazatlán, State Department officials at the Citizens Emergency Center confirmed that the body that was shipped to the United States was not that of Professor Schrock by calling the funeral home in the United States. The funeral home also referred them to "Dr. B" of the Denver County coroner's office who they said had performed a complete autopsy of the body.

"Dr. B" told the State Department officer that the body was definitely not Professor Schrock. He clarified that he and his two colleagues who assisted in the process, did not perform a full autopsy because the three experts determined independently through examination, measurements and x-rays that the corpse in question was not the one for which they had authorization to perform a complete autopsy. In their examination the three doctors quickly concluded that the body was older than Professor Schrock, had been dead longer than six weeks, had no dental work at all, and simply did not match Professor Schrock's medical records in any regard.

Officials at the State Department subsequently spoke with Dr. Geer and a relative of Professor Schrock. They said that they were following up with congressional offices on their request that professional investigators be assigned to look into the Professor's disappearance in Mexico. They also said they planned to hold a press conference the following Monday, July 19th.

The Embassy in Mexico City was able to reach Sinaloa Governor Antonio Toledo Corro by telephone in Mazatlán. Consul General Lane informed the governor that the body shipped to the United States was not that of Professor Schrock and demanded his government resume their efforts to locate the missing professor. The governor said his government would pay for the return of the remains to Mexico.

Ambassador Gavin, who was away from the Embassy, was also notified. He called Mexican Federal Attorney General Flores to let him know the United States expected a more energetic search. The federal attorney general reportedly asked that the fingerprints of the corpse in Denver be checked against FBI records and requested a copy of the Professor's fingerprints. Chargé d' Affaires ad interim (acting Ambassador) Perry Shankle made similar calls to the

Mexican federal Secretariat of Gobernación in Mexico City.

According to press reports, Mrs. Schrock held a news conference on July 17 at the Economics Department of the University of Colorado in Boulder where she said her husband had taught for 15 years. In an Associated Press article that appeared in numerous editions of newspapers in the United States and Mexico, Mrs. Schrock is quoted as saying, "Shipping the wrong body from Mexico was a vulgar outrage." She apparently added that "she hadn't decided whether the mistake was part of some plot or simply gross incompetence." The AP article went on to state, "I'm at a loss to understand why this body was shipped." and that the events of the past month, including a false alert on a body being found two weeks ago, had "heightened my sense of the absurd."

The State Department prepared the following press guidance for its noon press briefing on July 19th:

Q: Do you have any explanation of why the body returned to Mrs. Schrock was not that of her husband?

"A: The American Embassy at Mexico City has taken up this matter at the highest levels with Mexican Authorities. We have asked Mexican Officials to reopen their investigation as to the whereabouts of Professor Schrock. We have also asked Mexican Officials for full and complete details on how the body returned to the United States was misidentified.

If asked only (This means the spokesman should only use the answer if the question is asked during the daily press briefing.)

Q: What about the statement that Ambassador

Gavin has organized an "investigative team" to look into this matter?

A: You should direct that question to the American Embassy in Mexico City.

We had some contact with Mrs. Schrock that day in which she said she would send the dental records back to the Consulate in Mazatlán in case the Professor's body was "actually found". She said she would retain his passport.

In a related press issue, there was an unhelpful front-page article in the *Noroeste de Mazatlán* regarding an interview with San Ignacio Mayor Palacios. He was quoted as saying something like, "I don't understand what the concern is regarding Schrock's death in San Ignacio. Many Americans are murdered in Mazatlán every week." According to the article, he also disingenuously, and in great detail, asserted that everything done by the San Ignacio police in relation to the Professor's truck was proper and in accordance with Mexican law, which it was clearly not.

On either that day or the day before, principal officer in Mazatlán, Elayne Urban, spoke with Amy Shapiro, a reporter for the *Rocky Mountain News*. In an article appearing in the Denver, Colorado newspaper, on July 19th, Shapiro quoted Urban as saying, "We should keep this in perspective. It's easy to sensationalize, but it's only the murder of one man." In response to several letters from persons "expressing (their) outrage at the statements attributed to you (Urban) in the *Rocky Mountain News* of Denver ….", Consul Urban responded in part:

> While I had previously received oral reports of Ms.

Shapiro's article, I was shocked and angered to see for the first time that my brief conversation with her – in which I expressed sorrow and sympathy for the Schrock family over the (then) latest turn of events and my assurance of the Consulate's continued support and assistance – was distorted and misrepresented.

SUNDAY, JULY 18 — THE CONSUL GENERAL VISITS CULIACÁN

When it became clear that the body the Mexican authorities shipped to the United States was definitely not Professor Schrock, the Embassy in Mexico City decided to send a more senior Embassy Officer to Sinaloa to have direct discussions with that state's leadership. After consultations with his staff, Ambassador Gavin directed Larry Lane, the Consul General at the Embassy, to travel to Mazatlán on that day, July 18, for consultations with Consulate personnel and then direct discussions with the Sinaloa government officials in Culiacán. (The Consul General at the Embassy oversees all consular activities in Mexico. My boss, Principal Officer Elayne Urban, answered directly to him as did most of the other principal officers of the various consulates in Mexico.) Larry Lane's office then called Mazatlán consular staff to discuss logistics.

At his request, I picked up Consul General Lane at the airport in Mazatlán and we drove to the principal officer's residence for a briefing with her and with Vice Consul Michael Oreste. While Lane had an extensive knowledge of the developments in the Schrock case, we managed to fill in a few gaps and discuss state government personalities. As Principal Officer Urban had only just arrived at post and I had had frequent meetings with both the attorney general and the governor, Lane directed me to accompany him to Culiacán for the meetings.

Early on Monday, July 19, I picked up Lane at his hotel and we drove the roughly 125 miles on the old highway to Culiacán. It was very hot and humid as the rainy season was well underway. There were frequent potholes and heavy truck traffic. Still, we had a good conversation on the ride up. I told him what I knew about the governor, the attorney general and other senior officials in Culiacán. We also reviewed the various points we wanted to raise and the questions to ask. Consul General Lane emphasized that he would lead the discussions after I introduced him, but I should feel free to enter conversations, particularly with questions when I thought it prudent. It was good to hear that he had confidence in me, and he meant what he said. Still, I kept my interjections to a minimum as he covered the necessary ground during the meeting quite extensively.

Just after 10 a.m., we drove up to the modern, new state government building complex for our 10:15 a.m. meeting with Attorney General Jorge Chavez Castro at his office. He was waiting for us and ready to enter into discussions. Chavez Castro began by repeating his previous statements to the effect that Mexican law enforcement officials were convinced that the body shipped to the United States was of an American citizen killed by the San Ignacio police and who had been at the wheel of Professor Schrock's truck.

The attorney general said "logic" led to the identification of remains shipped to Colorado as being Professor Schrock since the police had confessed to killing the driver of Schrock's truck (thought to be an American since he was speaking English). In addition, according to the police, "he looked like Schrock's photo" and was wearing "American" clothing. The police also thought that he matched Professor Schrock's general build and height. The Mexican laboratory had matched the body's blood type with that of the Professor's, even though the Rh factor could not be determined. The attorney general could not explain why even a cursory examination by the Denver coroner, followed by a more extensive inspection, clearly indicated that the body was not that of Professor Schrock.

At about 11:15 a.m., a messenger interrupted our meeting with the attorney general to say that Governor Antonio Toledo Corro was ready to meet with us. Accompanied by Chavez Castro, we proceeded to the governor's office where we had a brief meeting with him. Also attending that meeting were the head of Gobernación, Jorge Robles Rendon, and the Secretary for Gobernación, Jorge Romero Zazueta (I knew Robles Rendon well but had only met Romero Zazueta once or twice before.) Governor Toledo Corro assured us that he and the state of Sinaloa would assist "in any way possible" in the search for Professor Schrock. He said that the Sinaloa authorities and law enforcement agencies were convinced that the body sent to Colorado was an American citizen killed while driving Professor Schrock's truck. (Based on our understanding of the results of the examination by the Denver coroner's office, we seriously doubted that possibility, but did not say so to the governor.) He suggested that the search should be renewed between Hermosillo and San Ignacio. The governor also repeated that his government would pay for the repatriation of the remains from Colorado to Mexico (which undermined his assertion that the body was that of a murdered U.S. citizen).

After we left the brief meeting with the governor, the attorney general asked if we would wait for him in Secretary Romero's office nearby while he took a few moments to talk to the local press. While Romero was quite cordial, we learned little additional information from him in the interim. As it turned out, Attorney General Chavez Castro had organized and scheduled a full press conference which detailed the findings of the Sinoloan authorities and the results of their searches and investigations. He repeated that the body shipped to Colorado was that of another American who the perpetrators had had murdered while he was driving Professor Schrock's truck. We were disappointed (well, actually, really annoyed) that the attorney general had used our presence for a press conference.

In any event, we then returned to Chavez Castro's office for a lengthy review of additional evidence. He showed us X-rays of the body (which his office had declined to provide us before the body was shipped), although these did not include X-rays of the head, which might have indicated dental work. The feet did appear severely arched. According to Mrs. Schrock, Professor Schrock generally wore arch supports.

We then examined a series of photos, some of which showed two policemen separately pointing out the burial site. The photos of the remains themselves show it appeared mummified, with the face quite decomposed. Had I seen it before shipment I would have had no idea as whether it was Professor Schrock or not. The body had been buried in the cemetery in a coffin. Authorities had not discovered how the suspects had secured the coffin, although the chief of police had been reported to have purchased one on May 9, 1982, well before Professor Schrock entered Mexico. In their confessions, the suspects had indicated the driver of the vehicle was murdered while wearing shorts and a short-sleeved shirt, but inexplicably, the killers had redressed the body in long pants and a long-sleeved shirt before burying it the first time. They also provided detailed information regarding the make, composition and type of clothing found on the body.

Chavez Castro had mentioned before in one of my telephone conversations with him that they had running glasses and a Casio watch belonging to the Professor, which agreed with the description provided to us by Mrs. Schrock. The attorney general clarified that these items had not been found with the body. They had been taken by the San Ignacio police from a box of books found in the Professor's truck and were later found in possession of family members of the police chief. The attorney general also asked if the Embassy could assist his office by sending him a copy of the report of the examination of the body shipped to Colorado by the three experts from the Denver's coroner's office. We suggested it be supplied to the Mexican Consulate in Denver who could then forward it to his office.

The attorney general then outlined his theory as to the crime. According to the policemen's confessions, the crime took place on the afternoon of June 1, 1982. Chavez Castro said an American had driven up to the gas station in Coyotitán and purchased 35 liters of fuel. According to this story, he did not get out of the vehicle, but showed the gas attendant a large roll of currency when he paid. (There was no evidence that Professor Schrock had more than a modest amount of cash with him as he had traveler's checks, but then again, Chavez Castro is saying this American was not the Professor.) As he left, he was followed by the deputy police chief, two policemen and the criminal "El Nene" all in a panel truck. They stopped the driver in the pickup near where the truck was abandoned. While the two police officers waited with the van by the highway, the deputy and "El Nene" drove the American up the hill, hit him in the head with a pistol, and strangled him with a wire. Before they killed him, he indicated he was an American. After they killed him, the two policemen joined them and helped redress the body and bury it. They left the vehicle near the highway. The next day someone reported the truck as abandoned near the highway and the police from San Ignacio retrieved it. At some subsequent point, according to the attorney general, the chief of police learned of the crime and had his policeman dig up the body and re-bury it in an old part of the San Ignacio cemetery.

The attorney general had little to add to this lengthy rendition but assured us his office would continue its efforts. He said he would later make a formal request for FBI assistance in searching for the fugitive "El Nene." After making a couple of other courtesy stops and finding a more private phone for Consul General Lane to report in with his office in Mexico City, we began the long drive home. After driving in thoughtful silence for a while, we began dissecting all that we had heard that morning. I told Lane that based on my previous experience in this case and what we had heard this morning, I didn't think that the body shipped to Colorado was an American, had been driving the pickup truck, or had anything to do with the disappearance of Professor Schrock. I added that I had no thoughts as to whether the San Ignacio police were involved in the disappearance. He nodded noncommittally, which was not surprising as he generally kept close counsel with his thoughts. We did, however, pick through the evidence point-by-point and discussed the various discrepancies or other puzzling assertions, like the redressing of the body.

About halfway back to Mazatlán, our conversation turned to, "OK, what next?" As the U.S. had no investigative jurisdiction in Mexico, we agreed on the need to continue pressuring Mexican authorities to enhance and broaden their search for Professor Schrock. We also needed to actively pursue the identification of the body shipped to Colorado. We would follow up with Schrock's family and the University of Colorado on expanding the newspaper ads offering a reward for information regarding the missing professor. We also discussed the logistics of returning the truck to Mrs. Schrock as well as the Professor's possessions once the Mexican authorities had no further need for them in their investigations. It was a good discussion, but we were both frustrated by the failure thus far to locate the Professor, and the apparent duplicity of senior Sinaloa authorities. After a long, hot, bumpy ride, we made it back to Mazatlán to check in with our colleagues and Consul General Lane returned to Mexico City the next morning.

Tuesday, July 20, was relatively quiet in Mazatlán for a change, at least concerning the search for Professor Schrock. We were still experiencing flooding from heavy rains as well as the normal heavy consular workload. Based on our and Embassy Mexico City's reporting, the State Department's Citizen Services Center notified the University of Colorado that the Government of Sinaloa would pay for the roundtrip expenses for the shipment of the body misidentified by Mexican authorities as being that of Professor Schrock. The funds the University of Colorado Foundation had sent to the Consulate in Mazatlán for repatriation of the body had not been disbursed and would be returned to the Foundation.

Several things of interest happened that Wednesday and Thursday. As he had told us he would, Attorney General Jorge Chavez Castro sent a formal request to Ambassador John Gavin requesting the assistance of the United States government in the search for Professor Nicholas Wickham Schrock. It specifically asked for all technical data and proof needed to identify Professor Schrock. The original was sent to Mexico City, but a copy was delivered to the Consulate in Mazatlán just before noon by a messenger from Chavez Castro's office.

The Embassy in Mexico City also issued a press release reading:

> During the past several days Ambassador Gavin has continued frank discussions of the case of Professor Schrock with high officials of the Mexican government, including members of the cabinet and the governor of the state of Sinaloa, Lic. (a title usually given to lawyers) Toledo Corro.
>
> At the Ambassador's request, Consul General Larry Lane has just completed a trip to Mazatlán and to Culiacán, where he met with Governor Toledo Correo (sic), and Sinaloa State Attorney General Chavez Castro. The United States government has renewed its offer of technical assistance made originally shortly

after Professor Schrock was reported missing and will facilitate the exchange of information between law enforcement agencies in the U.S. and their counterparts in Mexico.

The Embassy has been told by Mexican officials that their questioning of the seven men under arrest in connection with this case will continue and that the vigorous search for Professor Schrock will go on.

On Wednesday, July 21, the State Department in Washington, D.C., sent out a lengthy cable containing many, including some from Congressman Wirth's Washington, D.C., office, as well as a number of updates. In one of those bureaucratic complications that bedevils small posts in rural areas, the Consulate in Mazatlán did not receive the message in a timely fashion as it was classified as "Limited Official Use." While not technically a national security classification, the designation is generally used to protect personal information of American citizens and for other such matters. That designation has since been replaced by "Sensitive but Unclassified," and this particular message has since been declassified with some information redacted.

Because of the added protections, Consulate Mazatlán could not at that time electronically receive classified material or that marked "Limited Official Use". Important matters were printed in Mexico City and then delivered by courier when one was available. In any event, Mazatlán only found out about the message late in the afternoon when a consular official from Mexico City called to discuss how to answer the request. Most of the responses were contained in a July 23 cable from Mexico City.

The Department reported that after a thorough search of federal and state government records, including those of the Department of Defense, mentioned previously, the only fingerprint available for Professor Schrock was a print of the right index finger provided by the Colorado Department of Motor Vehicles. The coroner's office in Denver had also advised that the corpse of the body shipped to Colorado was too mummified for fingerprints to be taken. The only technically feasible way to try to get additional identification would be to sever the fingers and send them to the FBI's labs in Washington, D.C., for possible chemical analysis and print retrace. Since there was a high possibility that the remains were of a Mexican citizen, such a procedure could not be done without a formal written request from the appropriate Mexican authorities.

The incoming message also said the Department had not yet received the stained fabric samples from the truck that we had sent to see if they contained blood and they wanted tracking numbers. (The package was located shortly thereafter.) In addition, similar to the fingerprints above, since the stains were part of a criminal investigation outside the United States, the FBI would need a request from Mexican authorities to permit them to participate. We quickly confirmed directly with the FBI that the request for data and assistance which we had already received from the Sinaloa attorney general was broad enough to cover testing the stains.

The Department also wanted to know if Consulate Mazatlán had returned various items to Mrs. Schrock. We responded that I had transferred to her the personal papers he had when she visited on July 5th. (We are a bureaucracy, so she had signed a detailed receipt acknowledging acceptance.) We added that we continued to have possession of the truck and most of the items recovered with it. Some things such as the Casio watch, the shoe inserts, and running glasses were retained by the attorney general's office as part of their criminal investigation, but the attorney general had said they would return them to us once they had concluded their prosecution. The Department's message concluded by saying they were arranging securing a copy of the Denver coroner's report to be given to the Mexican Consulate in Denver and indicated that periodic updates from the Embassy and Consulates would be much appreciated.

The next day, Thursday, July 22, the Consulate in Mazatlán received a copy of a second request from Attorney General Jorge Chavez Castro for U.S. government assistance related to the disappearance of Professor Schrock. The formal request, addressed to Ambassador Gavin and dated that day, stated that at the petition of Captain Lozano Calva, director of the Sinoloan Judicial Police, his government would like assistance in locating and arresting Claudio Lamarque Pereda, aka "El Nene." The document had a detailed physical description and various photos of the suspect attached to it.

FRIDAY, JULY 23 – THE OTHER SHOE DROPS

It must be something about Fridays, but that was generally the day of the week when some startling new development manifested itself during the search for Professor Schrock. Friday, July 23 was to be no exception. Midmorning, we began to get calls from contacts and news sources saying that the body shipped to Colorado and identified by Mexican authorities as Professor Schrock was in fact Jesus Valenzuela Zamora, a 62-year-old bricklayer who died of a heart attack and was buried in the San Ignacio cemetery on February 4, 1982. We were unable to reach officials in the attorney general's office to confirm these reports but passed them onto Washington and the Embassy in Mexico City. While the entire search for Professor Schrock was laced with wild rumors, this one, for once, seemed credible.

A story on the front page of the *Noroeste de Mazatlán*, and also contained within an edition of the *Mexico City News*, reported that a family in San Ignacio had notified Mexican authorities that the body of a relative, Jesus Valenzuela, a bricklayer who died last February, was missing from his grave in the town cemetery. Sources reported talking with Alfonso Alarid Zamora, brother-in-law of the deceased, who apparently said that police officials dug up part of the family plot. The brother-in-law added that the deceased was 62, with black hair with just a touch of gray, black mustache and slight scars on the forehead. The press reports said the brother-in-law remarked that his deceased relative "had always wanted to go to the United States and now he had."

Our contacts within the state government (but not in the attorney general's office) told us that the new Director of Gobernación had ordered his officials to dig at other sites in the graveyard. On Thursday, July 29, in a telephone call with U.S. consular officials in Mexico City, Attorney General Jorge Chavez Castro finally admitted that the reports which identified the shipped body as that of a 64-year-old resident (sometimes noted as 62 years old) of San Ignacio who died in February 1982, were probably correct.

On Friday, July 23, the State Department issued press guidance for use on an "if asked only" basis on travel conditions in northern Mexico, which stated:

> Q: In light of the disappearance of Professor Schrock, what can you tell us about the safety of travel by Americans in Mexico?
>
> A: It is understandable that this incident has focused attention on travel conditions in Mexico. We consider the disappearance of Professor Schrock or any American citizen abroad a very serious matter and follow-up in any case which we discover or is brought to our attention. We have expressed our serious concern to the highest levels of the Mexican government. On balance, however, we should point out that hundreds of thousands of Americans visit Mexico each year without unfortunate incidents.
>
> Q: What precautions should travelers take?

A: The Department of State advises Americans travelling to any country to leave a detailed itinerary (including names, addresses, and phone numbers of persons and places to be visited) with relatives or friends so they can be reached in case of an emergency or traced if they do not maintain their expected schedule. If they change those plans, they should notify friends or relatives back home. Due to increased risk of loss while traveling, valuable jewelry, or objects which hold sentimental value should not be taken abroad. All travelers should not carry large amounts of cash or behave in a manner which would attract unwanted attention.

Q: Has the Department of State issued a travel advisory for Mexico?

A: No.

MONDAY, JULY 26 - THE SUSPECTS ARE INDICTED

The week began slowly in terms of the search for Professor Schrock. The rains continued flooding the streets. We didn't know it then, but we would be brushed by a fairly strong hurricane at the end of September that year. Most of our Schrock-related work early in the week focused on consultations with various parties about whether to renew the outreach for information with ads and whether the University of Colorado Foundation wanted to continue its reward offer. Consular officials in Guadalajara, Hermosillo, Mazatlán and Mexico City all recommended that at least the ads be continued. An article on the disappearance case also appeared in *Time* magazine for the first time, mainly noting the wrong body had been shipped to the United States and generally just reviewing the background of Professor Schrock's disappearance.

We later learned from Mexican government contacts and reports in the *Noroeste de Mazatlán* that on Monday, July 26, the cases against the seven ex-policemen detained in the disappearance of Professor Schrock were consigned to Enrique Estrada Lopez, Judge of First Instance in the Criminal Court in San Ignacio. This started a 72-hour clock under the Mexican Constitution for the accused to be formally indicted. The seven were also reportedly transferred to the jail in San Ignacio on the same day.

Most Mexican trials are largely paper exercises with few public sessions and those that take place publicly are normally relatively short. Judges then have a year under the Mexican Constitution to complete their investigation and pass sentence or release the suspects. The judge takes a more active role as a finder of truth rather than an impartial neutral party. While both the prosecutor and defense attorneys participate in the process, the judge has the key role. The Schrock case was to be an exception to the rule. On Tuesday, July 27, in a marathon public session that began around 10 a.m. and ended just before 2 a.m. the following day, the seven suspects were formally indicted. While one of the suspects continued to admit his participation, the other six recanted their confessions alleging they had been secured under psychological threats and intense physical torture.

Each of the seven suspects was questioned in turn and the indictments followed the essential outlines of the charges that the attorney general had described during the visit of Consul General Larry Lane to Culiacán. The police chief repeated in great detail his original story on how the truck had been spotted by a passerby and found abandoned by the police. Other than misuse of the vehicle and theft of some items from the truck, he denied any further knowledge of Professor Schrock's disappearance. Most of the other defendants made similar admissions. One of the defense attorneys argued strongly that the suspects could not be convicted of murder since there was no body and no evidence that the missing professor had been killed. Other defense attorneys opined that the mayor of San Ignacio should be indicted for his alleged misconduct.

On July 28, the Department of State issued the following

press guidance update on Professor Schrock which was submitted to the Department spokesman for the noon July 27 briefing:

Q: Do you have anything new on the whereabouts of Professor Schrock?

A: We continue to be in close contact with Mexican authorities and have impressed upon them the seriousness with which we view this matter. The Mexican investigation is continuing.

Q: What about Mrs. Schrock's request for a direct U.S. role in the investigation?

A: Only Mexican authorities are in a position to conduct criminal investigations in Mexico. Ambassador Gavin has, however, formed a working group of U.S. Embassy personnel in Mexico City to review information as it develops and to provide any possible assistance to Mexican authorities with their investigation.

On Thursday, July 29, Judge Enrique Estrada Lopez announced his ruling that all seven suspects would be held over for trial and denied bail. We learned from his office that the attorney general was trying to have the trial transferred to another court in Culiacán. Roberto Velazquez Treviño, deputy police chief of San Ignacio was charged with murder, robbery and assault. The other six are charged with concealment of the crime and, according to newspaper accounts, theft and illegal burial of a body. Attorney General Chavez Castro, in a call to the Embassy in Mexico City on July 29, confirmed the identity of the other six as: Arnulfo

Velarde Cruz (police chief), Ignacio Zuñiga Aguilar; David Antonio Valenzuela Osuna; Ismael Garcia Olivas; Lazaro Martinez Ontiveros; and Valentin Munguia Quintero. An eighth suspect, Claudio Lamarque Pereda ("El Nene"), who was believed by Mexican law enforcement officials to have killed Professor Schrock together with Velazquez Treviño, was still a fugitive.

State Department officials confirmed by telephone with Mexican Consul General Zamora in Denver that the body of the individual misidentified by Mexican authorities as Professor Schrock and shipped to Colorado would be returned to Mazatlán on Saturday, July 31 via a Mexicana flight. Consulate Mazatlán officials also confirmed the coffin was on the flight that arrived in Mazatlán at 5:30 p.m., although they had no involvement in organizing the shipment. Thus ended the second month in the search for Professor Schrock.

RISING CONGRESSIONAL CONCERN

Since June, when we were first notified of Professor Schrock's non-arrival in Guadalajara, we had been receiving a steady stream of letters from congressional offices (which State Department officials referred to as "congressionals"), family, colleagues and others expressing concerns over his disappearance. With each stage of the search, the finding of the truck, the false report of a second body, etc., interest grew. As one can imagine, after the shipment of the wrong body to Colorado and the indictment of the seven San Ignacio policemen, that correspondence increased dramatically. Given much of the narrative mentions congressional correspondence, I thought it useful to briefly describe the process at this point.

In general, congressional correspondence is just that-- written communications between either the Washington office of a Senator or member of Congress or from their district or state offices. The most common type involves their offices receiving a letter from a constituent that they forward under a cover letter to the relevant federal agencies for action or for a return explanation so that they can then reference such action or explanation in a reply to the constituent. At other times a Senator or member of Congress might have a particular interest in an issue or subject matter and write either for information or to try to influence a decision. Most of those dealt with by a Consulate, such as Mazatlán, involved constituent correspondence and consular matters.

Since Congress controls the budgets of agencies, an individual member of the Senate or House can have quite an impact on funding levels (or whether certain appropriations are even made), most federal agencies seek to respond expeditiously to requests from Congress. The State Department's goal was to respond to such inquiries in three days. This might not seem to be that quick, particularly when one was working in Washington, but that was a difficult goal when serving at a post far from the State Department.

As I mentioned earlier, the Consulate in Mazatlán got its electronic correspondence via an aging Western Union telex machine. However, at the time, most congressional correspondence, at least the incoming messages, were handled by regular mail or via the diplomatic pouch. The Consulate received regular mail and most of its routine messages, including congressionals, through a jerry-rigged system. Essentially items would be mailed to a post office box in Laredo, Texas where a State Department employee would gather them in large canvas bags, drive them across the border to Nuevo Laredo, Mexico and put them on a private bus for transport. (Some items were also shipped to us by air, but that was more expensive and so less often used.) This was a time when there was no internet and thus only rudimentary electronic banking that was expensive and not used for routine transactions. Thus, for example, try to pay a private bill owed to a company in the United States might take a round trip of 10-14 days. Outgoing mail was handled similarly, shipped by bus to the border, so payments made by those of us working in Mexico were often late. Another minor inconvenience for someone working in a rural outpost overseas.

So, during the early days of the search for Professor Schrock, and frankly throughout the entire search, the family and colleagues of the Professor engaged in a series of letter-writing campaigns to congressional offices and to the State Department, including the Consulate in Mazatlán directly. In early June we received a relatively small number of these, largely expressing the constituent's concern with the disappearance of the Professor and urging action. Most were directed to the Department, which routinely would send them to the post that seemed to be most directly concerned with the issue--in this case Mexico City, Mazatlán or Guadalajara. Most were initially directed to the Embassy in Mexico City which received its mail in a more timely manner. Even so, it took them some time to respond. For example, a July 1 letter from Senator John Glenn was only answered by cable on July 27.

Once the truck was discovered in Mazatlán, the Department began to send correspondence directly to the Consulate through the jerry-rigged mail system. That considerably lengthened the time for a response. Not only were the letters slow to arrive, often taking three to four weeks after they were written, but also we were understaffed. Drafting and responding to those messages took time that could have been used searching for Professor Schrock or helping other U.S. citizens. We would receive unhelpful messages from Washington asking why we had not responded to a congressional note that we had not received and would probably not receive for another week or so. In any event, our responses were slow even if we handled them as a priority. A typical example is a letter dated July 14 from Senator John Warner that we were only able to respond to on August 18. I am not criticizing Congress for its efforts to assist constituents or to provide oversight of federal programs and operations, but sometimes it did have unintended consequences.

The discovery of the truck slightly increased the number of congressional letters the Department received, but surprisingly the arrest of the seven policemen in San Ignacio and the shipment of the wrong remains, while again enlarging the amount of correspondence, did not do so quite as dramatically as I would have expected. However, the tone of the letters was understandably angrier and more outraged after the arrest and erroneous body shipment. In addition, the individual writers and congressional offices began to target more senior officials such as Secretary of State George Shultz and President Ronald Reagan.

By the end of August, we at the Consulate were really struggling to keep up with the correspondence. In addition, Mexico City was forwarding much of its mail to us. Toward the beginning of September, however, most of the correspondence was either sent to the Embassy in Mexico City or was answered directly in Washington. This made the Consulate's job a bit easier, although by then our work on the disappearance had slowed substantially. After Thunderbird and the University of Colorado began their fall session, the number of letters jumped again. By mid-November almost all of the congressional correspondence was being handled directly in Washington except for letters directly addressed to Ambassador Gavin.

In November we received many letters from members of Congress passing on concerns that a substantial number of other U.S. citizens had disappeared in Mexico and were probably murdered. There was little evidence given in the letters to back up these assertions, and the Department investigated all leads that provided even a small amount of information. On a closer look, most of the reports were erroneous. Where they were true--and there had been the murder or accidental death of several U.S. citizens--we were already aware of the deaths and had notified and assisted their families.

A notable exception to the routine inquiries and interactions with congressional offices during the search for Professor Schrock was the Department's interaction with Congressman Timothy Wirth and his offices. At the time he was the representative for Colorado's Second Congressional District, which included Boulder. He was later a U.S. Senator for Colorado and an Undersecretary of State under President Clinton. While he wrote a number of letters to the State Department, like other members of Congress, his staff was in frequent telephone contact with the Schrock family, the University of Boulder Foundation, the State Department, the Embassy in Mexico City and the various Consulates including Mazatlán. They were quite helpful as an informal conduit for passing information and ideas and, therefore, should be cited for their positive contributions to our efforts to locate Professor Schrock.

SUNDAY, AUGUST 1 - THE SEARCH CONTINUES

After the twists and turns of July, those of us working on consular issues in Mexico and Washington, D.C., were hoping that August would be better in terms of discovering what happened to Professor Schrock. June had ended on somewhat of a high point with the finding of the truck, but July, with Mexican law enforcement authorities indicating not once, but twice, that they had discovered Professor Schrock's body and even had us ship someone else's remains to Colorado, was a bitter disappointment. Still, we were determined to press on and were oddly somewhat optimistic that we would at some point at least discover what had happened to the Professor. We would work on what we could and continue to press the Mexican police and attorney general's office to renew efforts to find him.

Some things did begin to happen, albeit at a slower pace than anyone would have wanted. On Wednesday, August 3, the State Department reported that its liaison to the FBI had confirmed that the FBI lab had received the stained fabric samples from the Professor's truck as well as the July 23 formal request to test them. The lab had then expedited their examination and testing of the samples. I was not totally surprised to learn that the tests found no trace of blood present.

On that same Wednesday, August 3, in a telephone call

with Attorney General Chavez Castro, he told me that the "John Doe" body shipped to Mazatlán from Denver had been transported to Culiacán where it was being examined by doctors from Mexico City. He added that it was "not essential" for these medical experts to review the report prepared by the Denver coroner's office. Washington had told me earlier that day that the Denver coroner's report was still not in final written form, but since Chavez Castro viewed it as "not essential", I didn't pass on that information. I did, of course, tell him that the FBI had not found any evidence of blood on the stains from the truck. He took that on board but did not seem particularly interested in seeing a copy of the FBI's report. The attorney general ended the call by saying his office would continue the search, but at the moment, there were no new developments.

The first two weeks of the month -- in addition to our normal duties and maintaining daily contact with the Mexican legal authorities -- were largely taken up with fielding questions from the Schrock family and from Washington agencies. On Thursday, August 5, a consular officer transferring to the Consulate in Hermosillo was in Colorado on leave and was able to pick up a copy of the Denver coroner's experts report of the examination of the "John Doe" body from the Schrock residence in Boulder, Colorado. The Mexican Consul in Denver agreed to accept an original copy with the three signatures of the experts and then provide notarized copies for the State Department, the Embassy in Mexico City and to law enforcement officials in Mexico. The document was ten pages long and divided into three parts: forensic pathology, odontology and the radiologist's report. The U.S. consular officer also mailed a copy of the original to the State Department. Colorado Congressman Timothy Wirth's office, which as I noted earlier was in constant contact with the Schrock family and the State Department, advised that Dr. B from the coroner's office suggested that should another body be discovered in the future, assistance in obtaining a proper identification might be better obtained from the Armed Forces Institute of Pathology in Bethesda, Maryland than from the coroner's office.

The Schrock family member that handed over the report inquired about the return of Professor Schrock's truck to the United States. I had discussed the matter with Mrs. Schrock on several occasions and had told her that while somewhat bureaucratically complex, particularly as it was evidence in an ongoing homicide trial, it probably could be done in a couple of months. These things always take longer than one thinks they should. The family member had apparently spoken with the Mexican Consul in Denver about the matter who had pointed out the need to have the ownership papers and the temporary import permit the Professor would have received on crossing into Mexico. The Department asked if those documents were found by Consulate Mazatlán in the personal effects at Mazatlán. The Professor, like most people, had not traveled with his title, but we did have the temporary import permit.

On Friday, August 6, the State Department also inquired whether personnel at the Embassy in Mexico City or the Consulate in Mazatlán would be following developments in the criminal proceedings against the seven individuals in custody in San Ignacio and the one fugitive. When Mexico City Consul General Larry Lane was in Mazatlán, he and

Mazatlán Principal Officer Elayne Urban had discussed the matter and had agreed in advance that the answer should be, "Both" and to keep each other informed. Given the driving distances, this meant we might not be present at all hearings, but with notice we could make the more substantive ones. The Department's message also emphasized the importance of frequent and timely reporting on developments in the case, particularly in view of the regular calls from numerous congressional offices in Washington.

On Monday, August 9, in another call with Sinaloa Attorney General Chavez Castro, he repeated that there were no new developments in the search for Professor Schrock. Then he indicated an interest in obtaining assistance on polygraph examination of people charged with the murder of the Professor or suspected in the case. He also raised the issue of the use of sodium pentothal or other methods to force suspects "to tell the truth." He had mentioned the latter (sodium pentothal) in passing in a conversation we had had on July 28 and he now returned to the subject. I had discussed the matter in the interim with consular and legal officials in Mexico City and told him we had no information on whether sodium pentothal was available for use. I repeated that should his government be interested in either exploring the use of sodium pentothal or polygraph assistance, he needed to make a formal request for assistance that the Embassy would pass on to the appropriate law enforcement agencies in the United States. This was a fairly simple process that his office had already completed twice for other matters in the last couple of weeks. I also emphasized that any use of U.S. polygraph assistance would, of course, have to be "voluntary" and required the "cooperation" of the person being examined. The attorney general was to return to this issue repeatedly over the next couple of months, but never did submit the simple one-page formal request.

Toward the end of that week, the Citizen's Emergency Center at the State Department in Washington finally received notarized copies of the forensic reports prepared by the experts in Denver. Copies were forwarded to the Embassy in Mexico City and the Consulate in Mazatlán.

On Thursday, August 12, I called Attorney General Chavez Castro and asked him if he had received notarized copies of the forensic report from his government's consulate in Colorado. He said he had not. I had actually telephoned him to see if there were any new developments. In this case, there were two new items of interest. The attorney general said he had arranged for the trial of the seven suspects to be moved from San Ignacio to Culiacán. This would make it even harder for Consulate staff to attend trial hearings given the longer driving distances and often lack of advance notice of sessions. The case was now assigned to Judge Enrique Escalante Lopez, Chief Judge in the Criminal Court of First Instance in Culiacán. He confirmed that all the prisoners were still in custody and would be returned from San Ignacio, where they were being held, to Culiacán.

I am not sure why the attorney general wanted the case moved. He said it was so he could keep a closer eye on developments, but I suspected he also thought he would have more influence on the proceedings. The attorney general also acknowledged that forensic experts provided by federal authorities in Mexico City had confirmed the identification of the "John Doe" body as Jesus Valenzuela, the 64-year-old bricklayer from San Ignacio who had died in February.

One question raised by defense attorneys at the July 26 arraignment of the seven suspects charged in the disappearance of Professor Schrock was whether under Mexican law it was possible to convict suspects of murder without the production of the body in question. I had called several local attorneys and judges I knew in Mazatlán and raised the question with them. Most said that since the suspects were being tried in state rather than federal court, Sinaloa law would apply and under such law you could convict without a body if "other physical evidence was presented that showed in fact a crime was committed." One agreed to track down the legal citation and send it over to the Consulate as soon as he located it.

Three issues were to be the focus of our attention in the disappearance of Professor Schrock during the second half of August and the first half of September: 1) the truck, 2) the trial, and, 3) something else. First the truck. On Monday, August 17, the State Department sent Consulate Mazatlán a cable with the notation, "Forty-five Members of Congress Interested" but did not list them. The message was partially to clarify some outstanding issues regarding congressional responses that the Consulate was working to answer, but it mainly focused on the truck. We had not yet responded to the congressional correspondence as we had only just received it. Our telex machine was still suffering from sporadic outages, and it was our principal method of answering such requests.

The message also reported that two congressional offices had called the Department to point out that the Mexican auto insurance for the Professor's truck would expire on August 28 and Mrs. Schrock had told both congressional offices that she wanted to get the truck back before that date. That was, unfortunately, not going to happen, as I had told Mrs. Schrock on several occasions because the return of the truck required a great deal of paperwork and a number of permissions. First of all, as the truck was evidence in an ongoing criminal trial, we needed permission of the legal authorities (judge or prosecutor) to transfer it out of Mexico. We also needed a written request from Mrs. Schrock, supported by evidence of ownership, as well as permission from the State Department to make the transfer. Then, the officials at the Mexican side of the border would want a copy of the temporary import certificate, proof of Mexican insurance and possibly some document indicating the driver owned the vehicle or had the owner's permission to drive it. U.S. officials generally look at the license plate, and if they had any suspicion, proof of U.S. insurance and registration. There was also the question of who would drive the car. Our normal practice for recovering stolen vehicles and aircraft was to facilitate the request for recovery with the appropriate Mexican authorities and then have the vehicle transferred directly to the owner or his agent to actually return the vehicle to the United States. All of these steps were fairly straightforward, but all of them would require some time.

The next day we sent a long response back to Washington (with info copies to the Embassy and Consulate Hermosillo as we did with almost all messages involving the search for Professor Schrock). In our message we noted we had been working on the issue directly with Mrs. Schrock who had sent us a certified copy of a Colorado certificate of title, but it only listed Professor Schrock as owner and Colorado is not a community property state. We were unaware of any legal steps taken to either gain guardianship of his effects or to have the Professor legally declared dead. We therefore sought legal guidance and authorization to release the car to Mrs. Schrock or her agent absent clear legal title of ownership. It sounds like we were being overly bureaucratic, but as federal officers we were bound by oath to follow U.S. law. On the following day (August 19), in an unusually quick response from the State Department, we received very general authorization to release the vehicle to Mrs. Schrock or her agents, assuming Consulate Mazatlán would be "able to obtain all necessary documents to satisfy Mexican authorities at the border, where the vehicle is to be delivered to Mrs. Schrock or her representative." This was the bureaucratic version of "don't ask difficult questions-- just take care of things."

Our outgoing message on Wednesday, August 18, also noted that DFS officers under the command of Reyes Dominquez, headquartered in Hermosillo, were in the area to assist the local police in searching for Professor Schrock. They were in fairly frequent contact with both the Consulate in Hermosillo and in Mazatlán. The cable also reported:

> Journalists continue to call post for information, but primarily soliciting conjecture from post concerning the case. Post has declined to do so. One journalist told us August 17, 1982, that Chavez Castro said that the reason Mexican authorities failed to use dental records was because they arrived late. Chavez

Castro had the records in hand by 11:00 p.m. Monday, July 12 and did not make his official announcement of the identity until July13, 1982 at around noon.

And so it went.

On Tuesday, August 17, the State Department also sent the Embassy and the Consulate in Mazatlán a long cable classified as confidential that has since been declassified. It was a ten-paragraph message asking detailed questions about the trial and the investigation, many of which we had already answered. It didn't contain anything particularly sensitive or remarkable, other than an underlying sense of frustration with the lack of progress, but as it was classified, we couldn't receive it electronically. It was ten-to-fourteen days after transmission (that is, roughly at the end of the month) before we received a copy. The Embassy in Mexico City, of course, had it the day it was sent and after telephone discussions with Consulates Mazatlán, Hermosillo and Guadalajara, answered the majority of the questions on August 23.

On Wednesday, August 18, the attorney general called to inform post that another vehicle had been discovered abandoned in the area near San Ignacio. The vehicle was a 1972 Ford pickup truck, white-and-brown with California license plates. He formally requested that the Consulate check to see if the car was stolen or abandoned or if the owners were missing. It took a couple of days to track down the owners, but in this case, they were fortunately alive and well and had reported their truck as stolen in southern California. This was just one of many reports of abandoned or stolen vehicles that we received and followed up on over the next few months.

We also received a cable from Washington on Thursday, August 19, discussing the ad campaign and the outstanding reward offer. The University of Colorado Foundation was considering whether to launch a new ad campaign to publicize the search for Professor Schrock and the still outstanding $5,000 reward offer. In normal times, this was a large amount of money, but in August of 1982 it was particularly impressive. As I noted earlier, while we had been searching for Professor Schrock, the Mexican economy had been collapsing due to the falling price of oil. On August 12 the outgoing president announced that Mexico could no longer make payments on its foreign debt and on September 1, he nationalized all the banks. Inflation would exceed 100 percent in the next few months and the value of the peso plummeted. Suddenly $5,000 was quite a bit more money. The message basically asked if we thought it might be useful to run more ads, which we did and we let Washington and the Foundation know. With that done, we had a relatively quiet Friday and Saturday.

SUNDAY, AUGUST 22 TO MONDAY, AUGUST 23 - ALLEGATIONS OF TORTURE

On August 22, the president of the Sinaloa Association of Lawyers, Michael Jacobo, held a press conference in which he alleged the seven suspects from San Ignacio being held in connection with the disappearance of Professor Schrock had been psychologically and physically abused by agents of the Mexican government. He also released copies of medical reports detailing the alleged injuries to the suspects that had been prepared by the defense. He said that the individuals had been beaten and had received serious injuries during their torture by law enforcement authorities. The lawyer then said the prosecution's claims were riddled with inconsistencies and errors. While he admitted that some of the defendants might be guilty of theft, they were clearly not guilty of murder. Their alleged "torture constituted a violation of their human rights." The press conference was widely covered in the U.S. and Mexican press on August 23. One article in *Noroeste of Mazatlán*' quoted Jacobo as saying, "as far as I am concerned, Nicholas Schrock is still alive." But was he?

On August 23 the Embassy and Consulates in Mexico received the following message from the State Department that was rather frank in its tone:

The following CA press guidance entitled "Professor Schrock: An Update" was submitted to the Department Spokesman for the August 23rd noon Briefing:

Q: Do you have any comment on the charges by the President of the Lawyers Association of Sinaloa, Mexico that seven police officers in San Ignacio were falsely indicted to cover up an inept investigation into the whereabouts of Professor Schrock?

A: We are aware of the charges and expect that they will be addressed by Mexican officials conducting the investigation into the tragic disappearance of Professor Schrock. We have repeatedly emphasized to Mexican officials that we expect a serious and continuing investigation into Professor Schrock's whereabouts.

TUESDAY, AUGUST 24 — THE BODY FOUND?

On Tuesday, August 24, a new wrinkle, the third item referenced above, entered into our search for Professor Schrock. That morning we began to get numerous calls from our contacts, including a telex from Dr. Geer, that the previous day the Hermosillo-based newspaper, *El Impartial* had reported a body of "an American male about 40 years old" had been buried in the pauper's cemetery in Guaymas. The article said the deceased had been dead about two months when the body was buried. As Guaymas was in Hermosillo's consular district, we sent them a telex and later called them to see if they had seen the article (they had) and to offer assistance.

On Wednesday, August 25, Mazatlán Principal Officer Elayne Urban met with Sinoloan Governor Antonio Toledo Corro and other state officials in Culiacán as a part of her introductory calls. Not surprisingly, a major subject of conversation was the disappearance of Professor Schrock. The governor assured Urban that his state was continuing to investigate the matter with 20 federal and 20 state law enforcement officials in the field charged with finding the Professor. Our calls to confidential sources in Culiacán and San Ignacio confirmed that the state and federal police were, in fact, still looking actively, if not aggressively, for the Professor.

On Wednesday, August 25, we cabled Washington and the Embassy in Mexico City with more information regarding the transfer of the Professor's truck to the United States. By that time, we had received a copy of the title and insurance policy for the truck, but neither we nor Mrs. Schrock had been able to locate a driver willing to return the vehicle to the United States. The remaining paperwork looked fairly straightforward. Once a driver was found, the transfer should be completed quickly as the truck was in the possession of the Consulate and no Mexican authorities appeared interested in it. We subsequently received written notification from Sinoloan Attorney General Chavez Castro that he had no objection to its removal. However, legal sources in Mazatlán had told consular officials that the transfer might be more complicated under Mexican law if a Mexican citizen were to drive the truck out of the country.

Our legal colleagues in Mazatlán also found the legal site regarding conviction of murder without a body. Section 186 of the Sinoloan Penal Code (Código de Procedimientos Penales) printed in 1976 indicated a person may be found guilty of murder even if the body of the victim is not found if other evidence of a crime exists. The article reads:

> 186-Cuando el cadáver no se encuentre o por otro motivo no se haga la autopsia, bastará que los peritos, en vista de los datos que obren en el expediente, declaren que la muerte fue resultado de las lesiones inferidas.

The same legal authorities (local attorneys and judges) told us that the confessions of the accused, even if later recanted, are sufficient evidence of a death for the cited article to take effect. They added that the Supreme Court of Sinaloa had found this particular article to be proper according to both the state and federal constitutions. They also noted that Mexico does not allow double jeopardy in serious cases.

On Thursday, August 26, Consulate Hermosillo responded to our telex regarding the body in Guaymas and reported:

> We talked to the Dirección Federal de Seguridad on the twenty-third about this case. On the twenty-fourth they returned our call and gave us the following description: male, about 40 years old, five feet eight inches tall, blue eyes, light complexion, thick lips, bald and wearing only shorts. The authorities are assuming the body is that of a U.S. citizen because of the description and because no one locally fitting that description has been reported missing. The agent in charge of the investigation is Sr. Araiza, who is also in charge, locally, of the Schrock investigation. Sr. Araiza has told us that he will obtain dental casts or pictures and fingerprints for us. The individual had been dead for three or four days when discovered.

Subsequently, on August 30, Consulate Hermosillo reported by cable to Washington and the Embassy:

> Subj: W/W Schrock Disappearance Case
> 1. On August 23, 1982, A body was discovered in Guaymas, Sonora. Local authorities assume body is

that of USCIT because of physical description.

    2.   Body is male, about 40 years old, five feet eight inches tall, blue eyes, bald, light complexion, thick lips, wearing only shorts.

    3.   Agent in charge of investigation is Sr. Araiza of the Dirección Federal de Seguridad. Sr. Araiza is also in charge of local investigation into Schrock disappearance and is familiar with the case. He does not believe the body fits description of Schrock.

    4.   Sr. Araiza told Consulate he would obtain and provide dental casts or photographs and fingerprints. Consulate will check on possibility of obtaining photographs of the body.

The final item for the end of the third month of our search for the missing professor was a minor positive note. We finally located a driver to return the pickup truck to the United States. The driver was a U.S. citizen who specialized in recovering stolen aircraft and vehicles for insurance companies. I am not naming him or his associates, both of whom I had worked with on a number of previous recoveries of both aircraft and cars, in order to protect their privacy, even though this information was not redacted from the Freedom of Information Act documents I received from the State Department. Throughout this book I am leaving out the names of many private individuals, such as the doctor from the Denver coroner's office for similar reasons, even if they were named in documents released by the Department.

The driver generously offered to return the vehicle, or have one of his associates do so, just in return for the cost of gas and hotels, waiving his normal fee. Oddly, it took over four days to contact Mrs. Schrock and to get her approval, but she quickly sent up notarized documents authorizing the Consulate to transfer the vehicle to the recovery driver, and for the Mexican officials, permission for the drivers to transport the vehicle across Mexico. We would also provide the driver a similar letter in Spanish indicating the transport was being done with the knowledge and approval of the Consulate in Mazatlán.

SEPTEMBER

The discovery of a body in Guaymas was to take up much of the attention of those searching for Professor Schrock during the month of September, although most of the efforts would take place in Hermosillo's consular district by Hermosillo's staff, rather than Mazatlán's. Consulate Hermosillo reported the following on September 8:

> Following is an update on the body that was discovered in Guaymas on or about August 23.
>
> On September 2 we spoke with Cote. Beilis. [sic] Director of the Dirección Federal de Seguridad (Federal Security Force) attempting to get a description of the body. He said that it was impossible to get an accurate description because when the body was found it had been in the water for from five to eight days; was highly decomposed; and parts of it, including some of the face and fingers, were missing.
>
> We were originally told that pictures of the corpse were taken before it was buried but later learned that no photos had been made. The body was described to us at that time as weighing 100 kilos, 1.57 meters in height, bald, light complexion, blue eyes, from 50-55 years of age, and naked. Cmote Beilis (sic) also told us that the acting federal district attorney ordered the immediate burial of the body and that Dr. Jesus Telaza

Castro, a local physician, acted as the coroner.

Later we spoke to Mrs. Carmelita Yanez of the office in charge of civil registration in Guaymas, who is in charge of registration of deaths in that area. She provided us with the following information directly from the death certificate: the body was discovered in the Gulf of California on August [line of original text dropped] s male; is 60 years of age; had ruddy complexion; is bald; and died from drowning.

She said that no identifying information was found on the body. Miss [sic] Yanez said she would mail us a copy of the death certificate. She also informed us that in order to exhume the body to gather more identifying data, such as dental information, the Department of Health in Guaymas must be given an order to do so from what Mexican law refers to as an "interested party" and ask the Department of Health in Guaymas to exhume the body.

Since September 2, Hermosillo has been working with authorities in Hermosillo and Guaymas attempting to get the paperwork required to exhume the body. We were informed this afternoon that the body will be exhumed tomorrow (September 9) and that dental information and pictures of the body would be obtained. Post will furnish more details as they are made available.

As happens in most of these types of cases, the information often changes dramatically as the investigation progresses. Here the death notes the age to be about 60, not the 40-year-old estimate reported earlier. The height of 1.57 meters was also oddly precise. Some of the initial information had been relayed to Washington, Mazatlán, and Mexico City by telephone on September 2. The Department responded with a cable classified as "Confidential" but declassified on May 8, 1989, that said in part:

.... even though Mexican authorities (DFS Sonora's Sr. Araiza) apparently do not feel body could be Schrock's, dental records could lay this question to rest. According to Ref Telcon [a call between the principal officer in Hermosillo with the State Department's Citizens Emergency Center on September 2], the corpse does not have fingers or face; no autopsy was performed nor were any forensic records made prior to the burial; and death certificate lists age as 60 while press reports list age as 40.

.... Would appreciate Embassy requesting Mexican authorities to provide dental records on Guaymas body so that question of whether or not body is that of Schrock can be laid to rest.

On Friday, September 3, the Department sent a cable to the Embassy in Mexico City and the Consulate in Mazatlán -- classified as "Confidential" but declassified on May 8, 1989 -- addressing a meeting with DFS agents in Mazatlán regarding the disappearance of Professor Schrock. As the cable was classified as confidential, the Embassy responded for both Mazatlán and Mexico City with a partial summary dated September 4, again classified as "Confidential" but declassified in redacted form on May 8, 1989. (The redacted information is not included in any form in the information provided below.).

On September 2, four agents from DFS headquarters in Mexico City had appeared unannounced at the Consulate to discuss the case. Vice Consul Oreste and I met with them. They said they had already visited Hermosillo (the site of the DFS regional office for that part of Mexico) and Culiacán. They appeared well-informed regarding the case and said they had questioned the seven suspects being held in Culiacán. In an unclassified contemporary memorandum on the meeting that I wrote for our files, I noted:

> Based on their investigation, they indicated that they felt the seven San Ignacio police officials had nothing to do with the murder/robbery, but they were definitely guilty of misuse of the truck and theft of articles from the truck. The main agent said that he was 100 percent sure that the truck was on the hill for two full days after the incident, based on his questioning of the suspects.
>
> The agents indicated they felt that Schrock had left Hermosillo on May 31, 1982, early in the morning and that he was attacked at a detour point about three miles north of the truck discovery site. Further, they said that they felt he had never stopped at the gas station in Coyotitán.

We showed them Professor Schrock's truck and possessions and spent about 30 minutes briefing them on additional facts of the case. After they left, we called both the Embassy and the Citizen's Emergency Center to brief them on the developments. In its response to Washington (noted above) and in its conversations with the posts in Mazatlán and Hermosillo, the Department noted, "Disclosure at this time of the details of the DFS investigation would be damaging to the U. S. government's goal of a genuine resolution of the case." We didn't need the admonition as we were always careful not to disclose certain details of an ongoing investigation, although perhaps it was more useful in Washington where some reporting cables had been read to Mrs. Schrock and detailed in the press. Still, it was interesting that the DFS agents who had questioned the seven suspects did not feel that they were responsible for the disappearance of Professor Schrock.

In a related development regarding the body discovered in Guaymas, the Embassy asked us to pass on additional information to Mrs. Schrock. We were in daily contact with Mrs. Schrock and so the Embassy and Consulates generally passed information to Mazatlán to relay to the Schrock family. In this case, the Embassy asked me to brief her on recent developments including the somewhat gruesome details of the state of the body found in Guaymas. The Embassy also suggested that "she be told that if she wished comparison of Schrock's dental records with teeth of the body buried in Guaymas, consular officers would seek exhumation." Having interacted positively with Mrs. Schrock over the past few months, I was sure she would want a dental comparison done and to be provided with the results, which is what she then told me in our conversation.

Less dramatic actions were also occurring during this time. We conducted an informal, yet extensive survey, of our contacts in the area that found almost everyone was aware of the details of the disappearance of Professor Schrock.

We, therefore, reported that "post does not feel further publication of the reward notice through handbills or newspaper ads would produce any additional information. Post will, however, make every effort if the foundation thinks the effort warranted." There were then several administrative cables exchanged regarding accounting for the funds. The State Department reported that on September 9, representatives of the University of Colorado Foundation decided that it did not want to further advertise the reward officer at that time. They reiterated, however, that should positive information be received about Professor Schrock's whereabouts, the foundation would stand behind its offer. The Foundation officials also said they were pursuing further letters to Congress and noted Congressman Wirth's August 25 letter to U.S. Secretary of State George Shultz as an example of the results of their efforts.

Aspects of the trial of the seven suspects also continued to affect our daily workload. On Thursday, September 9, I received a registered letter addressed to me from Enrique Escalante Lopez, the presiding judge in the case against the seven suspects from San Ignacio. The letter said that the defense in the case had petitioned the court to ask whether Professor Schrock had any criminal record in the United States. It was a formal request that appeared in proper form, so I sent the contents by telegram to Washington with a positive recommendation that the information be sought and provided to the court. I also forwarded the original to Washington, with copies to the Embassy in Mexico City. It seems a routine matter, but it is important for the U.S. government to respond expeditiously, when appropriate, to proper formal requests for information so that foreign governments will also do so when we send them requests.

Unfortunately, nothing bureaucratic is simple. I was wrong about the request being "in proper form." The Department informed me on September 13 that to seek information in a criminal case, the petition needs to be in the form of a letters rogatory addressed directly to the U.S. Department of Justice. The principal officer therefore wrote a letter to the judge explaining exactly what was needed and I called him and walked him through the steps. Sometime later he sent us the letters rogatory that we forwarded to the Department of Justice.

On September 10, Consulate Hermosillo reported additional developments regarding the body discovered in Guaymas:

1. On Thursday 9 September Mr. Lopez Vasquez of Dirección Federal de Seguridad delivered documents ordering exhumation of body described in reftel [a cable referred to in the message, but not part of the text, in this case 82 Hermosillo 437] to Oficina Federal de Hacienda in Guaymas. Exhumation was originally set for five a.m.10 Sept. Sr. Barreto of Oficina Federal de Hacienda informed post today that exhumation has been postponed until 11 Sept. due to lack of available dentist.

2. Sr. Barreto stated an attempt will be made to obtain fingerprints if enough tissue remains to do so. Post had requested dental casts and charts be made in addition to photographs and dental X-rays. However, Guaymas does not have necessary X-ray equipment. Sr. Barreto stated that results of the examination will

be delivered to post on Monday 13 Sept.

On September 13 the Consulate in Hermosillo sent a follow-up cable:

> On September 13, Mr. Barreto of the Oficina Federal de Hacienda in Guaymas informed the Consulate that the body has been exhumed and that photographs have been taken. However, he was unable to locate a dentist who was willing to do the required dental work. Therefore, Mr. Barreto volunteered to receive instructions today and tomorrow Sept. 13 and 14, on how to take dental examinations, and he said that he would be able to complete the dental work toward the end of the week. Post will send updates as they become available.

In the meantime, on September 17, the Embassy in Mexico City and the Consulate in Mazatlán received a cable from the Department regarding some press reports of sightings of Americans. The Department noted that during its weekly call with members of the Schrock family, they had raised numerous questions, including one about a July press report which referenced the May 30 incident in Hermosillo where an American was hustled into a car. The family member did not think this was "the filling station incident" (also reported in the press) and wanted to know if the report had been investigated.

In addition, "regarding the search for the eighth suspect, Claudio Lemarque Pereda ("El Nene")," the family member noted reports in early July that "El Nene" had been sighted in Durango in the company of an American. The cable asked whether this reported citing was investigated and whether it involved helicopters. The cable also reminded all posts in Mexico that any information regarding the legal proceedings in process and the custodial status of the seven suspects, as well as "the status of search efforts, etc., would be welcome."

The Embassy in Mexico City responded on September 21 that although it couldn't locate its copy of the reporting cable from Hermosillo, the May 30 press article had been investigated by Hermosillo and DFS without developing any useful information. Hermosillo later clarified that they had been unable to investigate the report regarding a possible abduction of an American left by an unidentified woman caller on the after-hours duty-officer answering machine as both the machine was faulty and what information that was left was so vague that a follow-up investigation couldn't be made. The woman did not call back.

The Mexico City cable said the other questions were "probably best answered by Mazatlán." We replied on Tuesday, September 28 that, as we had reported earlier, the DFS agents had investigated the report of a sighting of "El Nene" in Durango around the first week of July and had not found anything. We also stated that despite their assertions at the time, DFS officials did not appear to have used helicopters in their investigation, at least according to contacts we had in Durango. We also wrote that we had a copy of Professor Schrock's dental records if Hermosillo still did not have them. (A copy was supposed to have been sent to them). The outgoing cable then reported on a telephone conversation with Attorney General Chavez Castro on September 27. The attorney general admitted that beyond the fact that the seven suspects were still in custody, he had little else to report.

Rather than relying on Mr. Barreto of the Oficina Federal de Hacienda who volunteered to be trained to conduct a forensic dental examination of the body found in Guaymas, U.S. officials at the Consulate in Hermosillo found an experienced dentist in that city willing to undertake the examination in exchange for a modest payment. On Wednesday, September 15, consular officials provided a car, driver, and Professor Schrock's dental charts to that dentist who traveled to Guaymas and performed the examination. Hearing of these developments on Friday, September 17, Mrs. Schrock asked the Embassy in Mexico City that she be provided with a copy of the results of any dental examinations conducted on the Guaymas body in order to independently compare them with dental charts for Professor Schrock. She had already mentioned that to me and I had reported her request to the Embassy.

Hermosillo's report of the results of the investigation read:

On September 20, 1982, [name redacted by author] the dentist who made dental casts of the body in Guaymas, provided Consulate with dental casts and a report of her examination. Her report is translated from Spanish as follows: Quote Hermosillo, Sonora 20 Sept, 1982. To whom it may concern: in the dental examination done on the cadaver which was exhumed from the municipal cemetery at Guaymas, Sonora, on Sept. 15, 1982, the following was observed: the lower left incisor and the lower left eyetooth were missing. The cadaver had all of the other upper and lower teeth, and it was noted that no dental work had ever been done on any of the remaining teeth. That means that during this person's lifetime, he never had any dental work done. I declare that the dentures of the cadaver do not correspond with the dental charts of Nicholas Wickham Schrock. Signed [name redacted by author] unquote. Copies of dental report being sent to Department of State; AmEmbassy Mexico City; AmConsuls Mazatlán and Guadalajara. Original copy of report and casts of teeth being retained in Hermosillo.

The Consulate's cable also clarified a discrepancy that the Department had noticed in the earlier description of the body. The proper height was 1.75 meters, not the 1.57 meters originally reported. It had been entered incorrectly by Hermosillo Consulate staff when they had been retyping the report into their aging Western Union telex machine. As in Mazatlán, all reports being transmitted required a laborious process of retyping the information into a long series of paper tapes and then feeding it into a reader.

Mrs. Schrock was informed that same day (September 21) that the body found in Guaymas was definitely not that of her missing husband. She said she was not surprised, based on the initial description, but was now more determined than ever to discover what happened to her husband.

The month of September was not going to end quietly for the consular personnel in Mazatlán. There were two major events, at least from the view of those serving there, yet to come. The first of these was a gathering storm, and this time, not a political one. While Pacific hurricanes only occasionally make landfall near Mazatlán, during the last week of September, a major hurricane was headed directly for the city and expected to arrive on the last day of the month. Coincidentally, September 30, was also the day that Ambassador John Gavin had decided to visit the Consulate in Mazatlán. This was part of the Ambassador's plan to visit all of the seven consulates that fell under his Chief of Mission status. This plan was not just the Ambassador's idea, but in fact, was made due to a criticism of his leadership made by representatives of the Office of the Inspector General (IG). The IG was conducting a routine periodic review of the Embassy and its constituent posts and flagged that the Ambassador had not visited more than one or two of his Consulates. He had then scheduled a visit about every 4-6 weeks and Mazatlán, as one of the smallest, was last on the list. His most recent visit to Guadalajara had reportedly not gone well, and he was quite unhappy with that post afterward.

While we, of course, welcomed the visit of the Ambassador, we were both exhausted from the high intensity work of the last 4-6 months (predating the disappearance of Professor Schrock) and concerned over the looming hurricane. Efforts to persuade his staff to postpone the visit, even for a week, were to no avail. The Ambassador was determined to come that day and come he did. We were, however, able to persuade his staff to limit his visit to one day (no overnight) which greatly reduced his time on the ground and the efforts needed to schedule him for that day.

Despite all of our concerns, Thursday, September 30, was a bright, sunny day. The hurricane had both weakened in strength and turned north so that it only brushed the city on the 29th. It had, unfortunately, caused major damage and loss of life further north. There were still major rains and flooding the day before in the Mazatlán area, but that had all cleared up by the time of the Ambassador's arrival on midmorning of the 30th. When he arrived, he was in a very good mood. Our fleet of aging vehicles managed to run all that day, although the Ambassador's security detail had driven a car up from Mexico City for him the day before.

Although the visit was not due to the disappearance of Professor Schrock, the issue was a necessary part of it. Sinaloa Governor Antonio Toledo Corro had driven down from the capital in Culiacán for the visit and brought several of his senior officials, including Attorney General Jorge Chavez Castro. They had a cordial and, from the Ambassador's side, very frank discussion of the need for Mexican law enforcement officials to do more to find out what happened to Professor Schrock. That was the only point during his entire visit that the Ambassador appeared visibly angry, which was useful in making his point.

The Ambassador also met with other local officials, such as the mayor of Mazatlán, who had been extremely helpful. The mayor and his staff appreciated this meeting with the U.S. ambassador and it helped us deal with future issues with his office. Finally, in a very small reception just for the American and Mexican staff at the Consulate, the Ambassador went out of his way to not just thank all the staff for their hard work, but particularly for the efforts to find Professor Schrock. Then it was time for the Ambassador to go. Rather than be driven right up to the plane – no connecting elevated skyways in those days-- he rather dramatically insisted on walking across the tarmac surrounded by his aides and security staff, climbing the steps, turning, pausing waving and he was gone. Yes, he definitely was an actor. Still, he always treated the Consulate and its personnel well and was a useful ally in the difficult times to come.

OCTOBER TO DECEMBER

The month of October ended up being much less eventful than the previous three, at least in regards to the disappearance of Professor Schrock. The consular workload in Mazatlán was just as heavy, but there were fewer developments in the search. While it may not seem so from afar, the visit of the sitting U.S. ambassador to a rural area like Sinaloa was big news. Even though he stayed less than a day, news of his visit was carried in all the major western Mexican newspapers, including those in other states like Durango, Sonora and Chihuahua. Much of the emphasis of the stories was understandably on the meeting with Sinaloa Governor Toledo Corro and the search for Professor Schrock. Stories on the ambassador's background and movie career also played a part. As for the ambassador himself, he wrote a brief cable to Washington regarding aspects of the Professor Schrock case classified as "Limited Official Use", but it was declassified on May 8, 1989. It read in its entirety:

> 1. During my visit to Mazatlán on Sept. 30 (for consultations with consulate staff), I met with high local and state officials. I asked about the Schrock case. The consensus among them was that the prisoners currently in custody may not be guilty. The officials all reflected puzzlement and bewilderment as to the whereabouts of the body and the identity of the

murderers. I stressed to them our interest in finding both the body and the perpetrator.

2. We will of course continue to pursue any leads and to keep the pressure on local authorities to resolve the case satisfactorily. Gavin.

The fact that the ambassador was reporting that Mexican officials did not think the seven suspects were guilty of murder (only misuse of the vehicle and theft) is telling. It's not so much that those officials told him that, but rather he is passing it along without any comment as to its validity or not, but not disparaging or questioning the assertion is interesting. It implies he agrees with this assessment. This reported statement by the Mexican officials raised several provocative questions: 1) If the authorities did not believe the evidence indicated the accused were guilty of murder, why were they prosecuting them for that crime rather than just theft and misuse of the vehicle?, 2) If they were guilty and had been, as alleged by their defense attorneys, tortured and physically abused repeatedly, why had they not revealed the location of the body? (Mexico did not have a death penalty for murder at the time.), and 3) If it wasn't them, then what happened to Schrock and where was his body? At the time I thought it likely that he had been robbed and killed near where the truck was found but if so, by whom and where was the body?

Other matters were more mundane. We continued to maintain pressure on the Mexican law enforcement officials to search for Professor Schrock and we also used other U.S. agencies working in Mexico to help in the search. For example, U.S. employees of the Department of Agriculture and the Drug Enforcement Agency would pass along any information related to the missing Professor that they came across. It was mostly rumors or possible sightings, but regardless of how credible, we would seek to independently verify them. While none of these efforts by other agencies led to the discovery of the Professor, on several occasions they tipped us off to developments or rumors well before the press or others learned of them, thus giving us an early chance to investigate and debunk them.

During the first week of October, the consul general in Mexico City, Larry Lane, returned to Washington, D.C., for routine consultations at the State Department. His meetings included discussions on the Schrock case with the Citizen's Emergency Center, the Mexico desk (the office at the main State Department in Washington that is responsible for bilateral relations with Mexico), and with representatives of the University of Colorado Foundation. With the latter he reviewed possible next steps in the search for Professor Schrock.

As a part of its efforts to search for Professor Schrock, officials at the Embassy in Mexico City had set up a practice of checking in with American Express and with the bank administering Professor Schrock's missing credit card. On Tuesday, October 12, we received notification from the Embassy that both institutions reported the day before that none of the travelers' checks had been cashed and there had been no activity on the Professor's credit card.

For some reason during this case, Fridays tended to be busier than other days of the week. On Friday, October 15, the judge overseeing the trial of the seven suspects sent the Consulate the letters rogatory in proper form and addressed to the U.S. Department of Justice asking whether Professor Schrock had any criminal record in the United States. We sent it by messenger to the legal attaché at the Embassy in Mexico City for forwarding to the proper office at the Department of Justice. We also sent the judge a formal note acknowledging the receipt and promising an expeditious reply. The Department of Justice had told us privately that they thought they could check available records and get back to the Mexican officials fairly quickly.

Coincidentally, on that same Friday, the State Department sent the Embassy and relevant consulates an update regarding additional steps regarding the reward offer. It turned out that after the early October discussions with Mexico City Consul General Larry Lane and other officials in Washington, the University of Colorado Foundation had changed its mind and wanted to undertake additional advertisement regarding its reward officer if the cost were reasonable. The foundation set the following stipulations:

A) The offer would emphasize that the source of any information received would be kept confidential.

B) The offer would make clear that the reward was from the University of Colorado Foundation.

C) The aim of the reward is to locate Mr. [sic] Schrock, not to prosecute anyone.

D) The advertisements would be spread from Mazatlán north to Hermosillo.

E) Prior to issuing the advertisements, Mexican authorities would be assured that, of course, information received would be shared with them to assist in their ongoing investigation; we would need to protect the source however, if any informant(s) so requested. The aim of the reward offer is to do everything possible to locate Schrock, not to interfere or usurp efforts of Mexican authorities.

The cable went on to request the Consulates' and Embassy's comments, proposals for advertisements, and cost estimates for a newspaper and handbill program. Before the end of the month, both Hermosillo and Mazatlán sent back lengthy cables regarding the print and advertising costs for handbills and ads in major newspapers in western Mexico. We also had lengthy telephone exchanges with the Embassy and Mexico City regarding optimal placement and timing for the campaign. The Citizens Emergency Center responded that further guidance would come from Washington after consultations with the University of Colorado Foundation.

Again on a Friday, this time October 22, five individuals arrived unannounced at the Consulate in Mazatlán to discuss the disappearance of Professor Schrock. While one individual identified himself as an agent for DFS, the federal investigation agency, the other four uncharacteristically refused to identify themselves or the organization they represented. In my time in Mexico, I remember very few cases when individuals, particularly those attached to law enforcement, refused to identify themselves. It was not only odd, but they acted somewhat suspicious, so we kept a sharp eye on them while they were there and attempted unsuccessfully to identify them after they left. This was just another of the unexplained developments in the search for Professor Schrock. In any event, they then asked to inspect

Professor Schrock's truck and made a thorough examination of it. They did not ask to see his possessions. They also raised various questions regarding Professor Schrock's background and his trip to Mexico and departed. We never heard from them again.

On Tuesday, October 26, the long-awaited day came, and the agent selected to drive the pickup out of Mexico arrived at the Consulate. Acting as agent for Mrs. Schrock, he took possession of the vehicle and we carefully loaded all of Professor Schrock's personal belongings into the truck. Even with the missing wine and clothing, it was a tight fit to get everything into the truck and the packing took some time. We also put the Colorado license plates back on the vehicle. The documentation was at last complete. Mrs. Schrock had arranged for insurance and had sent written notarized instructions allowing the Consulate to turn over the truck and possessions to the driver. The driver signed a receipt for the truck and possessions and had a notarized letter from Mrs. Schrock for Mexican officials. We also provided him with a similar letter to Mexican officials. In the interim, the Consulate had secured written permission from the Sinaloa attorney general stating the truck was no longer needed in the criminal prosecution and could depart Mexico. So much paperwork and effort for a simple transfer. The driver said he planned to drive the "Devil's Spine Highway" (a 200-mile, eight-hour drive over steep mountain roads) to Durango and then cross the border into Texas before proceeding to Boulder, Colorado where he would deliver the truck directly to Mrs. Schrock. After he drove off, I called Mrs. Schrock, which I had been doing on an almost daily basis at the direct instructions of Ambassador Gavin, and told her the transfer was complete and Professor Schrock's pickup truck and personal possession were finally en route-- almost four months to the day since we had located it in San Ignacio.

And so, the fifth month of our efforts to find Nicholas Wickham Schrock ended on a bureaucratic note with one last ripple. That same Tuesday, October 26, I reported to Washington and the Embassy in Mexico City a conversation I had had with a senior official from Thunderbird College. That individual had:

> ... contacted post concerning the possibility of having Dr. Schrock declared dead in Mexico for the purposes of clarifying workman's compensation, salary, benefits and other claims for the university. He indicated he would like something approved or verified by the Consulate.

AmEmbassy Mexico informs that under the Código Civil – Title 11, Articles 649 that the process of having someone declared dead in Mexico takes over eight years. First someone must petition the court. After 3-6 months the court will appoint a representative. Two years later the court will declare the individual officially absent, and six years after that he will be declared dead.

An examination of both Civil and Criminal Codes of Sinaloa indicated a similar section of the law for the State of Sinaloa. However, there seems to be no section allowing for a presumptive death, should a person be convicted for the murder.

After the intense efforts expended in the search for Professor Schrock during June, July, August and September, the fall was much quieter in that we developed few new leads. That was not for lack of effort. We continued to work with Mexican officials and to work our own contacts and those of other U.S. agencies to try to find out what happened to the Professor.

In my daily call to Mrs. Schrock on Saturday, November 6, she reported that the Professor's truck had arrived intact. She was satisfied with the condition of the vehicle and expressed her thanks to the U.S. government for its assistance in locating someone to drive it back to the United States. With that chapter closed, most of the efforts to locate Professor Schrock during the rest of 1982 revolved around a possible ad campaign. There were literally more than three dozen cables sent between the Department, the Embassy and the Consulates in Mexico during that time discussing costs and strategies for such a program. Rather than record those messages in detail, I will provide excerpts from a few of the more interesting ones. The Consulate General in Guadalajara, which was not mentioned in the October cable from Washington, stated that it would appreciate copies of any handbills printed regarding the reward for distribution in its district since the Professor had been destined to arrive in that city.

On Wednesday, November 10, the Consulate in Mazatlán suggested that in addition to a newspaper and handbill campaign that we also utilize radio advertising. We had been working on the feasibility of the idea for some time with the United States Information Agency's (USIA) office in Mexico City. At the time, USIA was an independent agency focusing on the media aspect of U.S. international diplomacy and communications. It has since been folded into part of the

State Department as its Public Affairs Bureau with overseas components in U.S. embassies abroad. As a result of the visit of one of their officers to Mazatlán in July to help with the press, the Consulate had been in frequent contact with their office in Mexico City. We would often exchange views on developments, keep each other informed on reports in the Mexican press, and generally collaborate on ideas. When we got the October message regarding renewing the Professor Schrock reward offer, we called them to strategize on the campaign. One of their officers noted that most Mexican citizens, particularly in rural areas like western Mexico, get the majority of their news from radio broadcasts and that might be a much more effective means of advertising the reward. We developed a plan with that office, including suggested content, and sent it by cable to Washington, the Embassy, and to other Consulates in Mexico. Although logically this sort of message would have come from the Embassy in Mexico City rather than the Consulate, for some reason the USIA officers said that it would be quicker and more effective if our Consulate sent it. I suspected at the time that for some unknown bureaucratic or personality-driven conflict, they felt it had a better chance of being accepted if the Consulate rather than the Embassy suggested the plan. A difficulty with being in a small, isolated post was that you were often unaware of bureaucratic currents elsewhere that might directly affect your operations.

Only a week later, on Wednesday, November 17, the Department responded positively to the suggestion to pursue radio ads, writing that the University of Colorado Foundation was interested in the proposal if it could be done in a cost-effective manner. It went on to make a few minor changes to the suggested text. The first paragraph of the message also noted that 54 members of Congress were now interested in being kept informed on developments in the disappearance of Professor Schrock. It authorized the placement of newspaper ads in Hermosillo that that post had suggested along with printing handbills. It ended by asking whether Mexican authorities had been consulted about the planned print and radio ad campaign. (We had not discussed the radio ads with the local authorities as we wanted to ensure Washington's concurrence before raising the issue.)

In a separate message, the Department tactfully suggested that since all decisions on the reward advertising campaign, which was growing in size and complexity by the day, were being made by the University of Colorado Foundation and since all cost and implementation information were in Mexico City, perhaps the Embassy could talk directly to the Foundation without the Department being an intermediary. A sound bureaucratic way of saying we have other things to do and it would be more efficient if you guys talked to them directly. The problem was that, for whatever reason, the Foundation had gotten into the habit of calling the State Department or headquarters directly even while having some contact with the Embassy and Consulates. Foundation members seemed to prefer having the Department intimately involved and resisted shifting their channel of communications to Mexico.

Various cables were sent over the next few weeks modifying the ad proposals and providing the fiscal data to permit the expenditure of the funds which were being paid for by the University of Colorado Foundation. One message from Mexico City on November 30 noted that Mrs. Schrock "does not want reference to her husband's body..." and asked the Department to confer with the Foundation regarding the matter. It also said that at the current exchange rates, a one-minute spot at most radio stations, repeated 75 times would cost less than 200 U.S. dollars. Thus, each radio spot was less than three U.S. dollars while a 1/8th page newspaper ad would run about thirty U.S. dollars. The Embassy suggested radio spots would thus be much more cost effective than newspaper ads and could be placed at five cities (Hermosillo, Ciudad Obregón, Los Mochis, Culiacán and Mazatlán) along Professor Schrock's intended route. It closed by stating that Consulate Mazatlán is consulting with Sinaloa state officials and the Embassy with federal authorities regarding the terms of the reward offer.

On Thursday, December 2, Consulate Mazatlán sent in the following message regarding the question of consulting the local authorities in advance of the reward advertising campaign:

> Post spoke with Lic. Jorge Chavez-Castro, Procurador for the State of Sinaloa concerning the reward offer by the University of Colorado Foundation. The general text of the offer and its conditions were discussed. Chavez-Castro indicated that if the offer would help to locate Dr. Schrock, it would be fine with his office. He also indicated that he had no objection to the assurance of confidentiality for sources of information. He repeated that neither he nor his office had any objections to any such reward announcement, nor any of its conditions.
>
> Chavez-Castro is aware that the offer is being

made by a private organization, the University of Colorado Foundation. He said he understood that the U.S. government was only acting to assist that organization but was not itself offering the reward.

Post has also discussed the reward offer with other state and federal officials, including agents of DFS and Roberto Robles-Rendon, the Director of Gobernación for the State of Sinaloa. Most of these officials, while not expressing enthusiasm for the project, indicated that they saw no problems with its implementation. Robles Rendon did say he thought the confidentiality assurance improper, indicating that all information developed should be turned over to the Mexican officials investigating the case, but he went on to state that he would not express any formal objections to the project.

I do not have any record as to whether officials at the Embassy in Mexico City had similar discussions with federal officials.

On Thursday, December 9, in a lengthy cable from Washington, Department officials were again passing on instructions from the University of Colorado Foundation to the Embassy and consulates despite the latter's efforts to maintain a more continuous direct channel to the Foundation. These instructions included cutting back on the newspaper ads and expanding the radio ads. My copy of this cable obtained through my Freedom of Information Act request has the handwritten note from Principal Office Elayne Urban to me stating, "Rob, who has responsibility for the radio spots? Mexico, Hermosillo or us?" Good question, but never satisfactorily answered. In the end, Consulates Hermosillo and Mazatlán coordinated directly with each other to place the radio spots within their consular districts as our efforts to have clarity from the Embassy on who was doing what were unsuccessful, although the Embassy negotiated and signed the underlying contracts. The message also noted that posts should use handbills as Mrs. Schrock thought they were effective. Before the end of the year, Consulate Hermosillo coordinated the printing of 5,000 handbills that were distributed throughout Mexico.

The cable also noted that 54 members of Congress were still interested in the case and that the Department was preparing a detailed chronology of the State Department's efforts to find Professor Schrock from his entry into Mexico on May 30 through the end of November. Each of the 54 members would receive a personalized response along with the 16-page chronology. The chronology had been prepared largely using the reporting cables from the various Mexican posts and the Department. The document was quite useful in organizing the material for this book. In addition to being a general message to the Embassy and the Consulates in Hermosillo, Guadalajara and Mazatlán, it had a separate paragraph addressed just to Mazatlán thanking post for its work on helping to prepare the chronology and for providing other information. It also noted: "(FYIO: Congressman Wirth's office advised DepOff today that Ruth Schrock had not heard from the Consulate since Thanksgiving and would appreciate a call." (DepOff just refers to the State Department officer in Washington that took the call from the congressman's office. It is short for Department Officer) We had not been neglecting her, but just had little to report.

In any event, I resumed my daily calls, although I limited them to weekdays. Let me also note, Mrs. Schrock had never requested daily calls, but only to be "kept informed." Ambassador Gavin was the one who directed me to call Mrs. Schrock daily.

On Thursday, December 16, something unusual happened, at least for a diplomat. I testified in court in the proceedings against the seven suspects in Culiacán who were charged with various crimes including the murder of Professor Nicholas Wickham Schrock. While it sounds a bit more dramatic than it was, I simply appeared in the judge's office and in the presence of the defense attorneys, prosecutors, and other officials (but not the suspects) was sworn in to make a brief statement. While it sounds fairly straightforward, it is extremely unusual for a U.S. consular or diplomatic official to appear in a criminal proceeding in a foreign court. International law protects such diplomats and consular officials from being compelled to testify and I had those protections as a part of my consular immunity. In addition, I had no individual power to waive such immunity to appear as that power resided in the State Department itself.

This appearance had developed over a course of several weeks. The judge's office had called and asked me to appear and testify that I had received a letter on July 22 from the attorney general, Chavez Castro, formally asking for U.S. assistance in the investigation. As I had received such a letter, I could so swear, but informed the judge that under international law, I would need the State Department's permission to do so. I said I would pass on the message and raised the issue with the Embassy in Mexico City. The

Embassy wanted to demonstrate our willingness to provide our assistance to the court in this case and so orally directed me to raise the issue directly with Washington, which I did. The Office of the Legal Adviser is the in-house counsel for legal matters for the State Department. It is the sole arbitrator of which international agreements the United States is bound by and is the office which oversees diplomatic and consular immunity, among many other things.

I called a friend I knew who worked in the Office of the Legal Adviser and they directed me to the appropriate official for diplomatic and consular immunity. I explained the situation and the Embassy's desire that we appear to be cooperating with the local judicial authorities. I told them the truth that I had no strong feeling one way or the other regarding testifying but would do so if they felt it advisable. It turns out that the Legal Adviser had no objection as long as it was clear that the U.S. government was only waiving immunity to answer a very specific question about the letter and that I was not available to, nor was I permitted to, testify on any other matters. They prepared the necessary instructions and authorization and the next thing I knew, I was in court. The whole proceeding only took about ten minutes. The final document had only two relevant sentences ratifying that the letters were sent and received. The rest of the document discussed who I was and the relevance of the issue I was swearing to. Still, it was interesting and provided me with a more comprehensive understanding of the bureaucratic nature of the Mexican criminal system (and the State Department as well).

My final recorded action -- although I am sure I was also following up with law enforcement and doing other things

-- for 1982 in support of the search for Professor Schrock was to write a letter on Wednesday, December 22 to Attorney General Jorge Chavez Castro. It was a year almost to the day that I had arrived in Mexico to take up my position as vice consul in Mazatlán and was after almost seven fruitless months of searching for the missing professor. The first part of the letter was to remind the attorney general that Mrs. Schrock would like the eventual return of her husband's watch, glasses and other small items recovered from the San Ignacio police that were part of the criminal case against the seven police officers. The second matter was "un poco más delicado" ("a little more sensitive"). The funeral home in Boulder, Colorado, had still not been paid for the receipt, storage and return of the "John Doe" body which his office had identified as Professor Schrock and had transported to the United States. I also sent a copy of the letter to Sinaloa Governor Antonio Toledo Corro who had told Ambassador Gavin directly that his government would pay for the costs. And so ended our efforts for 1982. We would return again to the search after the new year.

JANUARY AND FEBRUARY 1983

During the early 1980's the State Department was sending 400,000 cables a year to its posts abroad or more than 1,000 a day. On Tuesday, January 4th it sent one of its very first of the year to Mazatlán and other posts in Mexico requesting the status of the legal proceedings against the seven suspects detained in connection with the disappearance of Professor Schrock. It also asked whether the seven individuals were still in custody. This was a recurring theme as press reports and rumors persisted that the seven were not in jail. It took more than a week to make the various calls, which we would have done without the cable, to check on the status of the legal case and the detainees. We not only called Mexican legal authorities but also various contacts and sources, including other prisoners, that might have relevant information.

During that first week of January 3-7, I was on a routine prison visit and consultations trip in the north of our district and also stopped in to meet with various state officials in Los Mochis, Guasave, Guamúchil, Culiacán, and points in between the latter and Mazatlán. I passed out handbills regarding the reward offer en route to toll booths, gas stations and numerous other locations. Sources in the state government and private individuals in custody at the prison in Culiacán all said that the seven suspects were still in custody at the prison in Culiacán. Several of the suspects themselves reportedly said they thought that they would soon be released.

The general opinion of state authorities in Sinaloa (which I reported to the Embassy and to Washington) was that the seven suspects would be released "shortly." This, however, had been what these sources had been saying since mid-November. My discussions with judicial sources close to the case suggested that the judge was in the final stages of his investigations and deliberations. Several of his reported activities, i.e., sworn statements of certain witnesses, were apparently focused on winding up the case rather than the active pursuit of new information. While I reported this information, I doubted its accuracy as most trials took a minimum of a year, and even with all the political pressure on this one, I expected it to run the normal course and thus have the judge reaching a verdict sometime in late July or early August. I did not speak directly to the judge on this trip but intended to question him regarding timing at the first opportunity.

We also received a couple of congressional inquiries during January requesting status updates on the case that we quickly answered. The major activity of the month related to the search for Professor Schrock was the beginning of the radio spots regarding the reward. It took time to identify the best radio stations, negotiate contracts (handled by USIA in Mexico City the part of the Embassy that handled press matters), translate the text, record the spots, and distribute the tapes. It wasn't until almost the end of the month that we heard the first broadcasts. These continued through May 1984.

Toward the end of January, I made a routine pouch run to Mexico City and spent several days on consultations there. (A pouch run is when an embassy or consulate employee travels carrying the diplomatic bag including classified materials. These are not professional couriers, but employees with diplomatic or consular status sending in for the Department's professionals on a temporary basis. At the time the diplomatic bags we nonprofessional couriers carried were bright orange and sealed with a lead seal before they were dispatched. They were not subject to inspection, not even through x-ray machines by Mexican officials.)

Most of my discussions involved administrative matters as I was the Consulate's administrative officer, among my many duties, and it was becoming increasingly difficult to manage operations as the Mexican economy continued to implode. Due to the high, persistent levels of local inflation and the slow Embassy repayment process, the Consulate was constantly running out of money and having to decide which bills to pay and which to defer. We managed to keep the lights on and our vehicles running, but it was a constant distraction. However, on this trip I did spend several hours briefing the consular officers at the Embassy on the Schrock case and other citizen services cases as well as discussing methods to get the Mexican law enforcement agencies to renew their search for Professor Schrock.

In February, a new letter-writing campaign began under the impetus of the Schrock family and the Professor's former students and colleagues. This generated a substantial number of new congressional letters, many from senators and House members that had already expressed an interest in the case, but also included a significant number of letters written not to congressional offices, but by individuals writing directly to Ambassador Gavin in Mexico City. Almost all of this expressed frustration but provided little new information.

In mid-February, the Consulate in Mazatlán received another routine request for a status update on the case. It particularly asked if there was any evidence that Mexican law enforcement officials were actively looking for Professor Schrock and if there had been any developments in the legal proceedings against the San Ignacio police. We made a number of calls regarding the case and several sources confirmed the seven suspects were still in prison in Culiacán. State Attorney General Chavez Castro said that an initial determination of guilt had probably been made against some of the seven. The guilty sentence would be for misuse of the truck and homicide. The homicide would not be for killing Professor Schrock but for killing "the man driving the truck." I seriously doubted the judge would make such a ruling, although at the time I thought anything was possible in this case. I and emphasized in my report to Washington that the attorney general had not been a reliable source. Chavez Castro also told Vice Consul Oreste that an "amparo" had been granted for some of the suspects for some of the charges. An amparo, akin to a writ of habeas corpus, was a demand that charges be dropped and, if approved, the defendant would be released. Neither the judge nor the prosecutor acted favorably on the amparo.

Mazatlán's response also emphasized that similar to our January report:

> Mexican efforts to locate Dr. Schrock seemed to

consist largely of the trial investigation. There are indications that while most police agencies in the Sinaloa area are on the lookout for Dr. Schrock, none are actively investigating his whereabouts. The regional DFS office in Hermosillo filed its final report with their office in Mexico City in late November 1982. State agencies had covered little new ground since that time.

The report also stated that Mazatlán had received almost no responses to its handbill, newspaper ads and radio spots regarding the reward other than "one or two vague letters".

The report continued saying that consular officers in Mazatlán remained in contact with Mrs. Schrock with the most recent conversation only the day before the February 23rd message was transmitted.

On Wednesday, February 23rd I made the hot (even in February), grueling drive up to Culiacán for a routine visit to U.S. citizens in the prison there. I took the opportunity to confirm that, at least at the time, all seven suspects were still in custody. On February 24th, before driving back, I took the opportunity to call on the judge in Culiacán in charge of the case. We would often talk to judges about cases involving U.S. citizens, not to encourage them to rule one way or the other, but to both find out what was going on and also to push them to finish the trials within the one-year constitutional limit. Without such expressions of interest, a trial could continue for years and, at times, for longer than the period of the average sentence for the crime the defendant was accused of.

As expected, the judge declined to discuss the case in detail but did agree to comment on its progress. He said the defense was still pressing several legal maneuvers and he was not inclined to rush the defense in their motions. Furthermore, the judge added that he was still taking evidence as to some matters in the case. While he wouldn't give a date for his decision, he said he felt he would probably issue it sometime in April, six to seven weeks from the date of our conversation. That early date surprised me, but I didn't question him further on the timing. He added that all seven of the suspects were being tried on all charges, including homicide, and that evidence would lead one to expect some would be found guilty on at least some of the charges. He also said that he would inform the Consulate before making any decision public.

MARCH THROUGH JULY --
THE MANZANILLO SIGHTING

In early March, a U.S. citizen and his U.S. citizen wife who lived in Manzanillo came to the Consulate General in Guadalajara for routine passport services. Manzanillo is a Pacific coastal resort in the state of Colima and lies just under 200 miles by road south of Guadalajara. The American couple both saw the posted reward notice for Professor Schrock. They both stated they were certain they had met Professor Schrock in Manzanillo the previous year in May or June 1982. They said he was accompanied by one or two other men, both of whom they believed to have been Americans. The couple stated they would make further inquiries in Manzanillo and keep the Consulate informed. Consular authorities suggested they might want to communicate directly with the University of Colorado Foundation regarding the reward offer.

The couple returned to Manzanillo and, over the weeks, showed photographs of Professor Schrock to various residents. As there seemed to be a possibility of substance to the reports, the Consulate General in Guadalajara, whose district covered Manzanillo, volunteered to send an officer to that city to follow up. Instead, arrangements were made in mid-April for an Embassy officer from Mexico City to travel to Manzanillo in May to follow up on the sighting.

When interviewed by the Embassy officer, the U.S. citizen

couple confirmed the information they had previously given to Consulate officials in March. The male U.S. citizen described the person he believed to be Professor Schrock as between 40 and 50 years of age, slender build and wearing glasses. (This investigative trip was taking place roughly a year after the alleged sightings had taken place.)

The couple drove the Embassy officer to contact some of the people they said had positively identified Professor Schrock. The manager of a large hotel checked his records for a period of 8-12 months previously and came up with negative results. The manager showed the Professor's photograph to his security and maintenance personnel again with negative results. A different couple who were the owners/managers of a small hotel were also shown the photographs. The wife was "quite certain" she had seen Professor Schrock in the area several months earlier. However, she was unable to recall whether he had stayed at the hotel or if she had seen him in town. He was not listed in the hotel registry.

A woman residing in a pensión (a very small hotel) said she had seen Schrock three or four times in the Manzanillo area but could not recall when or where the sightings took place, only that they were within the last year or two. Four other individuals (owners or employees of supermarkets, ice cream parlors, etc.) claimed to have seen either Professor Schrock or someone that looked very similar to Schrock's photograph.

Perhaps the most interesting identification came from a man at a local restaurant. He immediately identified the photographs as being Professor Schrock. He said his brother had told him that he had seen that individual in the mountains just across the Colima state line in the state of Michoacán. The brother, when located and interviewed, denied having ever seen the individual in the photograph. The brother appeared evasive in his responses, and it was not surprising he did not wish to discuss his trips to the mountains in a marijuana growing area. The U.S. citizen later called the Embassy to say the mountain area he mentioned as seeing the Professor in was the Aguila-La-La Cita-Tecla area of Michoacán.

The Embassy officer concluded that either Professor Schrock or his lookalike had been seen in the Manzanillo area at different times and places during the year since his disappearance. That was an important conclusion that justified further investigation and coordinated efforts. In my view it also meant the Schrock family should be notified of these developments.

The Embassy decided to further investigate the area in Michoacán in the mountains and to furnish the Mexican authorities with the information that they had received. A slight snag developed as the Consulate and Embassy representatives had not secured a Privacy Act waiver from the U.S. citizen couple to release their names. They were eventually tracked down while on vacation in the United States and provided a waiver. (I am not including their names in this narrative to protect their privacy and because the identities are not particularly necessary for the story.) In its June 9 cable, the Embassy asked Department guidance as to whether it should inform Mrs. Schrock of the developments. That cable was the first time other Consular officials in Mazatlán and I became aware of the sighting as the April cable from Guadalajara had only gone to the Embassy in Mexico City without copies to either the Consulates in Mazatlán or Hermosillo. While we probably would not have been helpful in searching down a lead in Manzanillo, it is good general practice to communicate more broadly in case another post has something relevant to contribute. This sort of miscommunication, either deliberate or accidental, was going to consistently complicate the search for Professor Schrock.

Mrs. Schrock was not informed of the Manzanillo sightings until July 8, roughly four months after the initial visit of the American couple to Guadalajara and at least six weeks after the Embassy officer visited Manzanillo. The offices of Congressmembers Bernard Dwyer and Timothy Wirth both later complained to the Department regarding the failure to inform either their offices or the Schrock family in a timely manner. Mrs. Schrock asked for the names of the U.S. citizen couple and the Embassy officer that had traveled to Manzanillo in order to verify for herself the information she had been given. She received that information but spoke to Consul General Larry Lane rather than the Embassy officer who made the trip and later, with the U.S. couple's permission, Mrs. Schrock called the couple.

Monday and Tuesday, July 11-12, were extremely busy days in terms of cable traffic on the Schrock case. On July 11, the Department asked whether the mountain area near Manzanillo had been investigated. Mexico City replied the following day that photographs of Professor Schrock had been distributed, but the Embassy had not received any further feedback. Mrs. Schrock asked the Department to place newspaper ads, similar to those being published in western Mexico, in the Manzanillo area. She said she would pay for them. That same day the following press guidance was submitted to the Department's spokesman for the noon briefing:

Q: What information can you provide concerning the reported sighting in Mexico of Professor Nicholas Schrock, a University of Colorado Professor who disappeared in Mexico last Summer?

A: In March, 1983, an American citizen couple applying for passports at the American Consulate General in Guadalajara saw a posted handbill asking for information concerning Professor Schrock's whereabouts. The couple said they recognized the photo as that of a man they had seen in Manzanillo, Mexico in May or June 1982. The couple returned to Manzanillo and reported that other people in town whom they showed the photo recognized the individual. In May 1983, an Embassy officer visited Manzanillo and spoke with the American couple and several other persons concerning the whereabouts of Professor Schrock. One of those who thought she recognized the photo of Professor Schrock was the wife of the owner of a small hotel in Manzanillo. She said she had seen the man in the photo several months ago but could not recall when or where. Schrock's name did not appear on the hotel register.

Another woman who resided in a pensión (a small somewhat informal hotel) recognized the photo but could not recall any specific circumstances and said only that she recalled seeing the man during the last year or two. Four other individuals also said they recognized the photo but could not provide additional details. One man who was in a local restaurant said he recognized Professor Schrock's photo and said that his brother had also seen the man in the photo in the nearby mountains. When the brother was located and interviewed, he denied ever having seen the man in the photograph, i.e., Schrock.

The American Embassy in Mexico City reported this inconclusive information to the Department last month (June). No subsequent information has developed which sheds any more light on the whereabouts of Professor Schrock. The reported sightings could not be verified, and none of those questioned had any additional information. On July 8, the Department informed Mrs. Schrock of the leads and our unsuccessful efforts to follow them up.

Q: Why did we not inform Mrs. Schrock of this information immediately?

A: Before contacting Mrs. Schrock about these reported sightings of her husband, we attempted to substantiate the information. Although these leads were inconclusive, we nevertheless decided to inform Mrs. Schrock of our efforts to pursue them.

Q: Has Mrs. Schrock asked for more information?

A: Yes, she has asked for the names of the American couple who applied for passports in Guadalajara, and the name of the small hotel in Manzanillo where the owner's wife said she recognized the photo of Professor Schrock.

On Friday, July 15, Ambassador John Gavin sent a

diplomatic note to the Mexican Foreign Office [Secretaria de Relaciones Exteriores (SRE)] as well as letters to Sinaloa Governor Antonio Toledo Corro and senior federal officials in Mexico City notifying them of the information developed by the Embassy in Manzanillo and encouraging them to intervene personally to ensure that all possible steps were being taken to resolve Professor Schrock's case. These developments were only reported by cable from Mexico City to Washington, although (Mazatlán Principal Officer Elayne Urban forwarded a copy by letter to Sinoloan Attorney General Jorge Chavez Castro on July 18.)

Given the high level of congressional interest in the case, on July 20 a one-page information memo was sent from the Assistant Secretary for Consular Affairs to the Secretary of State alerting him that he might get congressional calls regarding the disappearance of Professor Schrock. The memo began by reminding the Secretary of the basic facts of the case and then proceeded to say:

A very tentative report that Professor Schrock was seen alive in Mexico during March of this year has recently received considerable publicity in Colorado and the Rocky Mountain states. Citing the March time frame, Congressman Timothy Wirth of Colorado has complained strongly to the Department that we have not kept him fully and adequately briefed on Schrock developments. He and Mrs. Schrock were not informed of the alleged sighting until two weeks ago. They were told they were not advised earlier because efforts to confirm the sighting indicated the report was baseless. Mr. Wirth is nevertheless convinced that the Department has deliberately withheld information from him and Mrs. Schrock.

In an effort to correct this impression, unclassified copies of the Department's cables on Schrock were sent to the Congressman on Friday, July 15. Congressman Wirth was still not persuaded. On Monday, July 18, his administrative assistant and two other members of his staff were allowed to read the classified cables in the Schrock file.

Given the lack of progress toward solving the Schrock case and the wide publicity which this case has received, we can expect more and persistent inquiries from Mr. Wirth and perhaps other members of Congress."

The State Department was still answering congressional complaints on the lack of early notification of Mrs. Schrock and the Embassy's slow action in investigating the Manzanillo sighting as late as October 12, 1983 (in a letter to Congress member Mary Rose Oakar). In similar responses to New Jersey Congressmembers Bernard Dwyer, dated August 15, and Jim Courter, dated September 24, Ambassador John Gavin wrote in part:

> The information concerning the reported sighting of Dr. Schrock given to you by ... is essentially correct. The Consulate General in Guadalajara was informed in March of this year by an American couple resident in Manzanillo, of their belief they had seen Dr. Schrock in May or June of the previous year. They were most cooperative and undertook to develop further information concerning the individual they thought to be Dr. Schrock. They notified the Consulate General by phone on April 15 that they had developed some leads but "nothing substantial." Nonetheless, the Embassy decided an experienced investigator should

visit Manzanillo and make a first-hand report. The report, dated May 20, was summarized to send to the Department of State by cable but transmittal was delayed while the Consulate General in Guadalajara sought to contact the couple and obtain authorization to identify them by name. Efforts to contact them were unsuccessful and on June 7 it was determined that he had left Manzanillo, reportedly for the United States. Their names were deleted from the cable and it was transmitted on June 9.

It seemed unlikely at the time, and continues to seem unlikely now, that Dr. Schrock was actually seen in Manzanillo. The Embassy believed it would be unsettling to members of Dr. Schrock's family and it served no useful purpose to notify them of the report before it had been carefully investigated.

The Embassy's report was received in the Department of State just when personnel there became engaged in assisting the University of Colorado in pursuing a lead on Dr. Schrock which had been generated by the reward offer made by the University of Colorado Foundation. The Department made the decision not to inform the Schrock family of the sighting stories until the University lead had been explored. By July 8, it seemed clear the lead was worthless, and Dr. Schrock's wife was informed of the Embassy report.

Although the Consulate in Guadalajara did post reward ads for information regarding the disappearance of Professor Schrock in the main Manzanillo daily newspaper, *El Correo de Manzanillo*, sometime after July 19, they apparently developed no new information, at least none that was reported. It appears from the above that by the end of July, the Embassy and the Department had decided that the reports of sightings of Schrock in Manzanillo were baseless and, except for the congressional correspondence, I found no further reference to the sightings after July. This is interesting because, although I personally do not believe Professor Schrock was ever in Manzanillo, the fact the Embassy officer investigating in May -- admittedly probably a year after the sightings -- thought the reports merited further efforts. Still, the month of July was once again a very active month for developments in the search for Professor Schrock.

Although there were developments in Guadalajara and Mexico City concerning the Schrock case during April, May and June, things were relatively quiet in Mazatlán, which was just as well given what was coming in July. At the beginning of the month, we received a wire note from the principal officer of the Consulate in Mérida. While dated March 28, we did not receive it until early April as our telex system had been down again. The different smaller Consulates frequently communicated directly and often notified each other regarding developments we might have missed. The wire note essentially repeated the contents of a cable from the State Department asking all posts in Mexico to review their files and send copies of all materials relevant to the disappearance of Professor Schrock to the Embassy in Mexico City, which we then did.

On Monday, April 18, Jesus Michel Jacobo, president of the State of Sinaloa Bar Association and defense attorney for six of the seven defendants being held for the murder of Professor Schrock, appeared at the Consulate. He spoke with Vice Consul Michael Oreste and me regarding legal developments in the trial. Michel Jacobo said that the six were pleading guilty to the theft from the truck, but claimed they had no part in the murder or disappearance of Professor Schrock. He also said that the defense had recently rested its case, and the judge would have to issue some sort of decision within 90 days. On questioning him regarding the judge's expectation of an April decision, he said he strongly doubted there would be a ruling anytime in April and probably also not in May given the additional judicial steps that needed to be taken. He said he would contact the Consulate the moment he heard anything more concerning the case. He added that he felt Professor Schrock was dead but declined to speculate as to who was responsible for the death.

On Tuesday, April 19, I again began the long, hot, bumpy, two-day trip for prison visits and other calls in Los Mochis in the far north of our consular district and to the capital city of Sinaloa, Culiacán. I confirmed that the seven suspects were still in custody in Culiacán and also checked in with various law enforcement officials, including the attorney general who had little to say except that the state had no ongoing investigation into the disappearance of Professor Schrock. My visit with the presiding judge added little new information. He would only discuss procedural matters, and now said he did not expect to reach a decision until sometime in early July. The defense attorney would become our most accurate source for information on developments in the legal case in the coming weeks.

During the week of May 30 to June 3, both the

newspapers *El Universal* and *The News* in Mexico City printed articles on the Schrock case. While discussing the disappearance of the Professor in general, the articles focused on the legal proceedings and the allegations of torture by the seven accused San Ignacio policemen. Both stories contained numerous factual errors regarding the sort of vehicle the Professor was driving and other aspects of the case. I suspected at the time that the defense was encouraging press coverage to try to show the suspects in a sympathetic light.

On Thursday, June 2, I called the defense attorney, Michel Jacobo, to see if he had heard anything new regarding the trial. He represented six of the seven defendants and had rested his case about 45 days previously. He said that the case was being delayed by another attorney, Ramos Campos, who represented the seventh suspect, Cruz Velarde. Ramos Campos had filed an amparo for his defendant. As noted previously, this is similar to a motion for habeas corpus-- a demand for the state to show cause for the detention or to release an individual. He said the amparo had recently been denied, but that this procedure had delayed the case for two months. He added that the other attorney had told him recently that he planned to rest his case on June 8, which would imply the judge would reach a decision during the first half of July. He said he thought the judge would find the men innocent of murder but guilty of theft from and misuse of the truck.

On Tuesday, May 31, in one of our routine calls, Mrs. Schrock said she would like assistance in placing a new series of ads in local Mazatlán newspapers. These would contain essentially the same information as previous ads and handbills. After the usual logistical back and forth regarding where to place the ads, how to pay for them and their composition, on June 22, during one of our regular telephone calls, she approved the final plan. On June 27, the first ad appeared in *Noroeste*, a major newspaper in Mazatlán. With the agreement of Mrs. Schrock, the next week ads began to appear in *El Imparcial* of Hermosillo. This ad campaign was to widen in the coming months and continued until May 1984 when Mrs. Schrock decided to end it.

As a result of the first ad, several stories and editorials appeared in Mazatlán concerning the case. Most of these merely commented upon the ads and the case. One editorial in *Noroeste* read, "We believe this to be an opportunity for the Mexican authorities to make amends for the (mishandling of the case) a year ago and, not because of a reward, but rather out of a sense of duty, to satisfactorily resolve the Schrock Case."

JULY – THE PROSECUTION ACTS

On Friday, July 1, we called defense attorney Michel Jacobo to see if there were any developments in the case. (He had thus far provided the most reliable source of information about the judicial proceedings.) The judge had limited himself to only discussing procedural matters and Attorney General Chavez Castro, while a necessary contact, was not reliable. Michel Jacobo said he felt there would be no further developments in the case until mid-to-late August. He was so sure of that, he added, that he was leaving on July 3 for a two- to three-week vacation in the United States. He did say he thought there was a possibility that the prosecution would drop the murder charges. We called Attorney General Chavez Castro to check on the status of the charges. He said he "had no plans of dismissing any of the charges." Chavez Castro added the verdict would probably be rendered before the middle of August and he would then have twenty days to review, and possibly appeal it before it became final.

On Thursday, July 7, Ambassador John Gavin traveled to Culiacán. In a meeting with Sinaloa Governor Antonio Toledo Corro, the ambassador stressed the need for state authorities to renew their investigations and actively search for Professor Schrock. The governor assured the ambassador that state authorities would take every step to discover what happened to the Professor. In the coming weeks there was very little evidence that they did so.

My assignment to Mazatlán was ending and I was to depart post on Tuesday, July 12. I was rapidly winding up my work there. I made my last call to Mrs. Schrock on Monday, July 11. We mainly talked about the continuing newspaper and radio ad campaign and about my successor, Douglas R. Smith. I gave her my regrets that we had met in such circumstances and gave her my continued sympathy. I also assured her if she needed anything, she could reach out to me at my next assignment in Germany, but she never did so. I followed up with a letter that covered the same ground but also provided additional information on my successor and the replacement for departing Vice Consul Michael Oreste, who had left post in late April. According to a memo to the files, Vice Consul Douglas Smith did not talk to her until August 9, when he told her that he had already asked the prosecutors for Professor Schrock's glasses and watch, which they had held in evidence.

On the morning of Tuesday, July 12, with the car packed up and me saying final goodbyes to my colleagues in Mazatlán, as I was preparing to drive out of the city, the phone in my office rang. It was the Attorney General, Jorge Chavez Castro. In a long, rambling monologue, he informed me that the prosecution would soon rest its case and was recommending sentences of 16-30 months for theft and misuse of Professor Schrock's vehicle. (He was vague on exactly who was receiving each sentence.) He said his office was, by the way, dropping all assault and homicide charges for lack of evidence. In this way, should further evidence be found, such as the Professor's remains, the charges could be refiled. I organized my notes, briefed Russell Frisbie, the other new vice consul, and Principal Officer Elayne Urban and drove off.

Apparently, the consular officers reported this development to Mexico City by phone but did not file a cable report to Washington until July 29. The timing had been unfortunate. With my departure and the defense attorney out of town, it took quite a bit of time for the Consulate to verify developments and discover that on Wednesday, July 13, the day after he called me, the Attorney General had formally rested the prosecution's case and dropped the charges of homicide.

On Tuesday, July 19, shortly after he returned from vacation, defense attorney Jesus Michel Jacobo, as he had promised, sent a copy of the prosecution's formal decision addressed to me at the Consulate. As he was in Culiacán and sent it by regular mail, it did not arrive at the Consulate until Monday, July 25 and it took some time for staff to realize what it was and the implications. In addition to being in Spanish, it was written in legalese, and at times difficult to decipher. On July 27, Principal Officer Urban called the Citizens Emergency Center in Washington to let them know that the prosecution had formally dropped the charge of murder and most of the suspects would receive a sentence equivalent to time served. The Department immediately called Mrs. Schrock and another family member who asked what steps the Mexican authorities would take in the case and what resources would they throw into a renewed investigation. They also wanted copies of the prosecutor's decision.

In preparing this book, I carefully reviewed all of the original Spanish language court filings in the case along with affidavits and sworn testimony and decisions. The seven legal-page length document, dated July 13, was signed by a prosecution official from the attorney general's office. It reviewed the evidence and concluded that the material evidence necessary to sustain convictions for the crimes of homicide, assault, secret burial, and coverup was lacking against those seven defendants charged with those respective crimes. (Not all defendants were charged with each crime.) The recommendations further concluded that the material evidence necessary to sustain convictions for theft had been proven against three defendants, Roberto Velazquez, Ismael Garcia, and David Valenzuela. It further state that there was sufficient evidence to convict all seven defendants for (violation of) official responsibility.

The document provided some rationale for the dropping of the various charges, including the lack of a body and the recanting of confessions by most defendants. With this document, the state was formally dropping most charges and also making sentencing recommendations to the judge should he decide to convict the defendants on the remaining two charges. The judge had twenty days from the date of the recommendations (July 13) to render a final decision on the remaining charges.

The following press guidance was submitted to the Department spokesman for use in the noon briefing of July 29, 1983. (No questions on the Schrock case were raised that day.)

Q: Is it true that Mexican officials have dropped murder charges against the seven policemen being held in the Schrock case?

A: We understand that the prosecuting attorney in a recommendation reviewed by the Attorney General of Sinaloa had recommended that the homicide and assault charges against the individuals being held in the Schrock case be dropped. We also understand that they have concluded that there is evidence sufficient to convict three of the men on theft and all seven of misconduct charges. This is a recommendation of the prosecuting attorney, not a ruling from the judge. I have nothing more for you on this at this time.

Q: What sentence will they receive?

A: I cannot speculate.

Q: What is the department doing to ascertain the whereabouts of Professor Schrock?

A: The Department, through our Embassy and consulates in Mexico, continues to work with the Mexican federal, state and local officials to ascertain the whereabouts of Professor Schrock.

Q: Do you have any comment on the letter sent to Secretary Shultz and President de la Madrid of Mexico by Congressman Wirth and other members of Congress urging the resolution of the Schrock Case?

A: The Department shares with members of the Schrock family, friends, and colleagues, as well as the Members of Congress who signed the July 25 letter, their frustration at the lack of progress in determining the whereabouts of Professor Schrock. I have no specific comments on the letter.

JULY - CONGRESS REACTS

As the press guidance in the last chapter noted, on July 27 the State Department in Washington received two letters, one addressed to Secretary of State George P. Shultz, and one addressed to Mexican President Miguel de la Madrid Hurtado. In a development I had not seen previously nor since in my long diplomatic career, both were signed by 75 members of Congress, including the Speaker of the House, Thomas P. O'Neill, Jr. It was undeniable that there was substantial interest in the disappearance of Nicholas Wickham Schrock. The Secretary had been briefed on this possible development in an information memorandum dated July 20. The letter to Secretary Shultz, dated July 25, 1983, reads:

> Dear Mr. Secretary:
>
> We are writing to bring to your personal attention the case of a prominent U.S. citizen whose disappearance in Mexico more than a year ago remains unresolved. The Government of the Republic of Mexico has so far failed to provide a satisfactory explanation or mount a thorough investigation despite the efforts of three U.S. Consulates, the United States Embassy in Mexico City and the Department's Citizens' Emergency Center in Washington.
>
> Because this case can only be resolved by a comprehensive investigation by the appropriate

Mexican federal agencies, we believe it merits your personal attention and contacts between our governments at the highest level.

Professor Nicholas Schrock, a respected member of the faculty of the University of Colorado at Boulder, disappeared May 30, 1982, en route to participate in a program of visiting professors at the Autonomous University of Guadalajara. His vehicle and personal effects were later discovered by U.S. consular officials – acting on a tip, rather than on information provided in response to repeated inquiries to responsible state and federal agencies – in the possession of local officials in San Ignacio, a small town in Sinaloa State along the InterAmerican Highway. Local officials had appropriated the vehicle for their own use.

In July, 1982, six members of the San Ignacio police, including the chief of police, and one civilian were arrested on charges including murder and robbery. Federal and state investigations appear to have ceased soon afterwards, and no body was ever recovered. On July 15, 1983 the murder charges were dropped by Sinaloa State officials.

To date, neither Professor Schrock nor his body has been located. In view of Sinaloa State's decision that the evidence in the case against the seven suspects was insufficient to support a charge of murder, we believe it is incumbent upon the Mexican government to reopen investigations by federal agencies which were terminated last summer. The Government of the Republic of Mexico no longer has any explanation to offer for Professor Schrock's disappearance.

We have communicated this request directly to President de la Madrid in the enclosed letter, which was delivered to the Ambassador of Mexico in Washington today. We strongly urge you to make a similar urgent request at the cabinet level on behalf of the Administration as quickly as possible.

As we stated in our letter to President de la Madrid, our foremost concern is that Professor Schrock be located, or at least that Mrs. Schrock and his family be provided the most complete information possible regarding his fate. They have already suffered through more than a year of uncertainty, disappointments and indignities at the hands of Mexican officials.

Other matters remain to be resolved as well. Cooperation by Mexican state officials with our consular officers in this case has been sadly lacking, and in some cases the information provided has been misleading, or worse. We urge you to review the history of this case thoroughly and make clear to the Mexican government that the United States Government expects law enforcement officials at high levels to offer the same cooperation and assistance to American consular officers that we provide to Mexican consulates in the United States. Otherwise, the thousands of Americans who visit Mexico each year cannot be assured of their safety while traveling in that country.

We strongly urge that you communicate our government's insistence on a comprehensive federal investigation of this matter to the Government of the Republic of Mexico at the earliest possible opportunity.

We look forward to hearing from you.

Over the course of the next month or so, there were another six-to-ten congressional letters written to associate the writer with the July 25 note or to press some other issue regarding the Schrock case, including a more personal "Dear George" letter to the Secretary dated August 1 from Senator Barry Goldwater. The accompanying letter to President de la Madrid, also dated July 25, was similar in tone and content to the letter to Secretary Shultz. It reads:

His Excellency Miguel de la Madrid, President of the Republic of Mexico.

Your excellency: we wish to ask for your personal assistance in a matter which we regard as being of grave importance in the relationship between our two nations. A full year of efforts by the United States Embassy in Mexico City with officials of both the Mexican federal and Sinaloa state governments has not resolved the situation, despite diplomatic contacts at the highest levels, and our confidence in the government of the Republic of Mexico is in danger of being seriously undermined.

Professor Nicholas Schrock, of the University of Colorado at Boulder, disappeared on May 30, 1982, en route to participate in a program of visiting professors at the Autonomous University of Guadalajara. His vehicle and personal effects were later discovered by U.S. consular officials in the possession of local officials in San Ignacio, Sinaloa, who had appropriated the vehicle for their own use.

In July, 1982, six members of the San Ignacio Police, including the Chief of Police, and one civilian, were arrested on charges including murder and robbery. On July 15, 1983 the murder charges were dropped.

To date, neither Professor Schrock nor his body has been located, and it appears that neither Sinaloa state nor federal agencies are actively undertaking any further investigation of the case. Particularly in view of the termination of the murder prosecution of the seven suspects in Culiacán. No satisfactory explanation for Professor Schrock's disappearance has been offered to the government of the United States. In addition, the case raises serious questions regarding the conduct of state government officials during the original investigation, in their administration of justice and towards U.S. consular officials.

We request that you direct the appropriate federal agencies to reopen their investigation of Professor Schrock's disappearance as quickly as possible. Our foremost concern is that he be located or at least that Mrs. Schrock and other members of his family, who have suffered deeply over the past year, be provided with the most complete information possible regarding his fate. Simple humanity requires no less.

Beyond this concern, serious questions have been raised regarding cooperation between our two governments in the protection of U.S. citizens in Mexico. This case has received widespread publicity in the United States. A thorough federal investigation is absolutely essential if the thousands of Americans who visit Mexico each year are to be assured of their safety while traveling to your country.

We believe this matter to be of such seriousness that it merits your personal attention. We respectfully await your reply.

I don't know if President de la Madrid ever replied to the letter. However, on August 3 and 4, the Embassy in Mexico City sent out direct personalized cable replies from Ambassador John Gavin to the 75 members of Congress who signed letters on July 25 to President de la Madrid and Secretary Shultz. They read:

> I have received copies of the letters you and other members of Congress sent on July 25, 1983, to President de la Madrid and Secretary Shultz concerning the disappearance in Mexico of Dr. Nicholas W. Schrock.
>
> I share your extreme frustration over the failure to resolve the mystery of Dr. Schrock's fate since his disappearance on May 31, 1982. From the text of your letter, I know you are aware of the intense interest and efforts made by the Embassy and our consulates at Mazatlán, Hermosillo, and Guadalajara to resolve this case. Our strong concern continues.
>
> The indictment on July 29, 1982, of seven policemen from San Ignacio, Sinaloa, on charges including the murder of Dr. Schrock, caused us to hope that the facts would be definitely established in the ensuing judicial process. Officers at the Embassy and the Consulate at Mazatlán closely monitored this

process, conferring frequently (within the bounds of Mexican law and procedures) with the judge, chief prosecutor and defense attorney. At the same time, we maintained contact with Mexican state and federal law enforcement authorities, urging that they continue their efforts to resolve the case. I stressed to the Governor of Sinaloa in our meeting at Culiacán on June 7, 1983, the great importance the United States government, and I personally, place on obtaining a satisfactory explanation of Dr. Schrock's disappearance.

On July 12, an official of the state of Sinaloa told us that the prosecution had decided sufficient evidence did not exist to establish the responsibility of the defendants for Dr. Schrock's death, and that the murder charges were being dropped (this action preserves the possibility of later prosecution for murder, should new evidence become available).

I was disappointed in this development, which means that little or no progress has been made in the past year to determine what happened to Dr. Schrock. I immediately informed the Governor of Sinaloa and the Federal Secretary of the Interior of my views, urging that they ensure that necessary action be taken to solve this distressing case. The Embassy sent a Diplomatic Note to the Mexican Secretariat of Foreign Relations with the same message.

I and other Embassy and Consular personnel are continuing to press the appropriate Mexican authorities. We are also investigating leads presented on the whereabouts of Dr. Schrock. Currently we are checking out reports he has been seen in Hermosillo and Manzanillo. We are keeping Mrs. Schrock informed of developments and responding to her requests and suggestions. We are coordinating closely with Dr. Schrock's colleagues at the University of Colorado and the American Graduate School for International Management.

I assure you that our efforts and interest will not flag as long as this case goes unresolved.

JULY – THE JUDGE DECIDES

There were even more events to take place in July before the month's end. On Friday, July 29, a year to the date of the indictment, Judge Enrique Escalante Meza pronounced sentences for the seven defendants in the criminal proceedings deriving from the disappearance of Professor Nicholas Wickham Schrock. This was going on at the same time the Consulate in Mazatlán was reporting on the prosecution's dropping of murder and other charges and while the Department and Embassy in Mexico City were responding to the congressional correspondence signed by more than 70 senators and members of the House. The fact that the trial was taking place at a substantial distance from the Consulate in Mazatlán and the persistent failure of Mexican law enforcement and judicial authorities to notify the Consulate of developments, meant consular officials were unable to attend the court hearings and decisions in this case.

On Saturday July 30, the Consulate sent a "NIACT" immediate cable to Washington. NIACT stands for "night action," meaning that if it were received after hours, certain people should be awakened to act on it. The message reported that:

> This morning's (Saturday July 30, 1983) edition of the local daily *Noroeste* reports that all seven former

police officers accused in the Schrock case were freed yesterday afternoon around 5:00 p.m. local times. The article states that the seven defendants were found guilty of theft and (violation of) official responsibility.

The cable went on to state that the Consulate was not officially notified of the reported sentencing and would contact the authorities to verify the press reports and seek an explanation as to why the seven suspects were released even though they were found guilty.

On Wednesday, August 3, the Consulate in Mazatlán further clarified the judge's decision. The message read in part:

> On Friday, July 29, 1983, Judge Enrique Escalante Meza pronounced sentences for the seven defendants in the criminal proceedings derived from the disappearance of Nicholas Wickham Schrock. As reported previously, the judge considered only the cases made by the prosecution for theft and (violation of) official responsibility. The cases for homicide, assault, secret burial, and cover-up having been dropped by the state. The sentences were as follows:
>
> 1. Roberto Velazquez Treviño, guilty of theft and (violation of) official responsibility, two years, 3,900 peso fine;
>
> 2. Ismael Garcia Olivas, guilty of theft and (violation of) official responsibility, one year and ten months, 3,900 peso fine;
>
> 3. David A. Valenzuela, guilty of theft and (violation of) official responsibility, one year and nine months,

3,900 peso fine;

4. Ignacio Zuñiga Aguilar, guilty of (violation of) official responsibility, one year and four months, 3,500 peso fine;

5. Valentin Munguia Quintero, guilty of (violation of) official responsibility, one year and four months, 3,500 peso fine;

6. Lazaro Martinez Ontiveros, guilty of (violation of) official responsibility, one year and four months, 3,500 peso fine;

7. Arnulfo Velarde Cruz, guilty of (violation of) official responsibility, one year and five months, 3,200 peso fine.

State Attorney General Jorge Chavez Castro read the data above over the telephone to ConOff on August 2, 1983. Chavez Castro then explained that when a sentence of two years or less is rendered by a court, any defendant so sentenced is automatically eligible for "conditional liberty." The terms of such "conditional liberty" are totally within the discretion of the presiding judge and generally include the posting of bond, periodic presentation of the defendant at court offices, and some restrictions on travel. The defense attorney for six of the defendants, Jesus Michel Jacobo, confirmed the date above, and added that Velazquez, Garcia and Valenzuela posted bonds of 20,000 pesos each, and that Zuñiga, Munguia, Martinez and Velarde had posted bonds of 10,000 pesos each in order to secure their "conditional liberty." Defense lawyer Michel insisted that, apart from the bonds, the judge had placed no further restrictions on the defendants' "conditional liberty." After the time remaining on the defendants' respective sentences has passed, the bond monies will be returned (to the defendants).

Both Chavez Castro and Michel Jacobo promised to forward copies of the sentences to the Consulate. We shall pouch further copies to the Department and to AmEmbassy Mexico upon receipt.

By letter dated July 29, 1983, to Chavez Castro, ConOff requested return to AmConsulate Mazatlán of any personal effects of Nicholas W. Schrock no longer needed by the court or prosecution.

As he said he would, on Tuesday, August 2, Michel Jacobo mailed the Consulate in Mazatlán the lengthy sentencing summary and conclusions of the judge, which arrived at the Consulate on Monday, August 8. Michel Jacobo was a consistently reliable source of information and documentation. I have reviewed the original Spanish copies of the six-page sentencing summary and the 33 pages (legal-sized paper) of the judge's deliberations and conclusions and found the Consulate's reporting to be an accurate summary of them. It's not that I didn't trust their work, but rough translations of complex legal documents made under time pressures and compressed in size for cable traffic are sometimes unreliable. A more careful and leisurely review is often necessary to gauge accuracy.

The seven convicted men were then essentially released for time served (one year), put on a sort of parole for the remainder of their sentences, and fined. With the collapse of the Mexican economy in 1982 the peso had fallen sharply in value. By July 29, when the judge made his decision, it was trading at roughly 160 pesos equal to one dollar. This means that the highest fine was roughly $25 U.S. dollars and the highest bail (20, 000 pesos) was equivalent to about $125 dollars. To my knowledge, that was the end of the involvement of the seven convicted suspects in the case. While there were some calls to reindict them for murder or on federal charges, to my knowledge they were never again charged and after their sentences ended, they largely faded from the case.

AUGUST THROUGH DECEMBER

After the fires of July burned down and the activity regarding the trial began to diminish, there did not appear to be many developments for the rest of the year. There was a real question of "What next?" I had left Mexico and, therefore, was not part of the internal discussions. After apparent consultations with the Schrock family, the University of Colorado Foundation and the State Department, the Embassy in Mexico City the Consulates appeared to have continued the dual strategy. They maintained a newspaper and radio ad campaign for information regarding the missing professor -- along with a reward to try to find more information regarding the Professor's disappearance. They also appear to have renew efforts to push the Mexican federal, state and local law enforcement authorities to resume their search for Professor Schrock.

While there is ample evidence in the files for a renewed ad campaign, despite expressions of interest from the highest levels in Washington and Mexico City, there is no indication of any new efforts by Mexican authorities to resume an active investigation. At the same time, the Mexican economy continued its rapid decline with soaring inflation, a collapsing peso, and severe supply chain disruptions complicating daily life in Mexico.

There were some interesting developments, some of which began in July. On Monday, July 18 and again on Tuesday, July 19, the Consulate in Hermosillo received anonymous telephone calls from a woman who was interested in knowing if the reward for information about Professor Schrock was still available. She said she might have information but refused to provide her name or telephone number.

On Thursday, July 21, a woman who identified herself as (name redacted by author) called to tell consular staff that she had seen Professor Schrock wandering the streets of Hermosillo. She said she had followed him and called him "Nicholas." He then turned and looked at her but walked away. She added that the man appeared to "have a mental problem." She refused to leave a telephone number or address, but said she was going to look for him again and contact the Consulate later. She said she had seen his picture in the local newspaper (reward ads were run locally on July 10, 17 and 24). She was definitely interested in the reward but did not provide any further information, such as a physical description of the man she saw.

On Friday, July 29, a man and the woman who had called earlier appeared at the same Consulate and, after identifying themselves, said they were positive that an American-appearing man who has been wandering the streets of Hermosillo for several months was Professor Schrock. They showed a picture they had taken of the individual, which was taken from a distance and showed the individual's back. They said they had tried to follow this man to learn where he lived but were unsuccessful. They added that they tried to speak to the man on several occasions, but he appeared reluctant to converse. The woman said she had sent a cable to the University of Colorado on July 28 and was called back by an official there who said someone was coming to Hermosillo to talk to her further. The consular staff asked the man and woman to notify the office should they see the man again. Staff were informed to keep a lookout for the individual who the Consulate then tried to locate. In addition to reporting this information to Washington, the Consulate also sent the contents to Congressman Wirth's office as he had repeatedly asked to be kept informed.

On Saturday, July 30, the Department cabled Consulate Hermosillo to report that the official from the University of Colorado had called to say he had received a cable from a woman in Hermosillo asking for someone to call her regarding the search for Professor Schrock. One of his Spanish-speaking colleagues called her back. The woman said there was a man in Hermosillo whom she believed to be Professor Schrock. He was thinner and bearded. She had taken a picture of him but unfortunately from behind. The man appeared confused, disoriented, ragged, and slightly crazy. The report from Hermosillo and the cable from Washington had crossed each other, as the Department ended with a request to interview the woman and report back, both actions the Consulate had already completed.

Several staff members at the Consulate in Hermosillo said that they had also seen the individual that the local woman and man had reported sighting. All staff members were very familiar with the physical description of Professor Schrock, and all said that the man appeared to be too tall to be the Professor (estimates ranged from six feet to six feet, two inches as opposed to Professor Schrock's reported height of five feet, nine inches.) Even though the man's description did not seem to match that of Professor Schrock, witness descriptions can be unreliable. The Consulate contacted the local authorities in charge of the Schrock investigation who agreed to follow up on the reports. The Consulate also sent its staff to several areas where the individual had been sighted.

On Friday, August 12, a consular officer spoke with the woman and the man who thought they had seen Professor Schrock. Both now said they were convinced the man they had thought was the Professor was not him. They said they had received additional descriptive information from someone in Denver that convinced them the individual was not the Professor. The following Friday, August 19, the police called to say that the individual sighted was apparently known as "Kent" and had not been seen lately. People they interviewed who said they knew him indicated they believed he had returned to the United States. The police were trying to find "Kent's" full name and U.S. address. The Consulate reported that although it appeared virtually certain that the individual sighted was not Professor Schrock, they would continue to try to locate and identify the individual.

Further south, on Friday, August 19, an American citizen who declined to be identified appeared at the Consulate General in Guadalajara. The man said that based on a photo on a reward handbill he had seen, he was positive that he had seen the several times in a local bar. Consular officers then went to the area identified by the informant and located the bar, the "Aristos Mascusa II," a working-class establishment. The bar was described by the officers as being within walking distance of an area of Guadalajara frequented by numerous

U.S. citizens whom the local police described as alcoholics. The consular officers did not see any individuals appearing to be American citizens in the bar, nor the area, except for the informant who appeared to be on his way home. No one at the bar recognized the photos of Professor Schrock. Copies of the handbill and a more recent photo of Professor Schrock were left at the bar.

According to the informant, the photo of a younger Professor Schrock with a short haircut closely resembled the man he had seen at the bar. The man was seen accompanied by an older man and they would visit the bar in the afternoon to drink beer. The informant thought the man appeared to be between 35 and 40 years old, no glasses, brown hair, ordinary teeth and ears, with a slight build. The man claimed to be an ex-ballplayer for the San Diego Padres but didn't have the physique of a professional ballplayer. He reportedly spoke average English with no trace of an accent and had no visible marks or tattoos. He also seemed to have a good education and some sort of beef with the Veterans Administration.

The consular officers tended to discount the report as the informant insisted Schrock looked more like the "younger Schrock" photo and his general description did not seem to match what was known of the Professor. They reported their findings to Washington asking the Department to contact Mrs. Schrock to see if anything the informant said would leave her to think the man described in the bar was her missing husband. On August 31, Department officials contacted Mrs. Schrock and briefed her on the Guadalajara sighting. She said she doubted the man frequenting the bar was her husband but would be grateful if someone could continue to try to find the man and determine his identity.

Over the ensuing weeks consular officers returned to the bar several times to try to locate the man identified by the informant to no avail. The bar manager consistently stated that she had not seen the individual in the photos but would keep the handbill and call the Consulate should the man appear. In a letter dated October 27, 1983, to Douglas Smith, my successor in Mazatlán, Mrs. Schrock again noted that she doubted the person seen in Guadalajara was her husband. The letter went on to thank my successor for sending her the glasses and watch that the San Ignacio policemen stole from the Professor's truck and which had been returned by the Sinaloa attorney general. She said the Professor had had the glasses for more than 20 years and they had a special meaning to her. She was not as familiar with the watch, but it appeared to resemble the one he took with him.

Just when it looked like the rumors and sightings could not get any more bizarre, the mystics arrived. On Friday, October 14, Douglas Smith wrote a memo to Consul General Larry Lane at the U.S. Embassy in Mexico City reporting that within the past week two "psychics" had offered unsolicited advice as to the whereabouts of Professor Schrock. The first arrived at the Consulate and explained that he could determine from a photo whether the subject was alive or dead. He was provided with one of the reward handbills and passed a compass-like device suspended from a silver metal cord over the photo. He then pronounced the Professor dead. Following this, he traced a lead pencil over a map of the state of Sinaloa, ultimately defining an area roughly 10 by 15 kilometers (map attached to memo) and said the remains of the body were within that designated space. The "psychic" added that even if he could travel to the area, it was too large for him to locate the body. He also said he was not interested in the reward. The area on the map enclosed a very large section roughly west and north of the area where the truck was found.

The second "psychic" wrote directly to officials at the University of Colorado who then sent the note to Mrs. Schrock who forwarded a copy to Vice Consul Smith. The original was handwritten in Spanish and was translated at the University of Colorado. That translation, which appears to me an accurate recording of the original that I reviewed, read:

> September 19, 1983
> University of Colorado
> Dear Sir:
>
> Do not search to find the Dr. alive that you are now looking for – in the search where his car was found from North to South and to the right a few meters from where his car was found-in that place he is buried- this was done to rob him– when you find his body look for me, I do not want the reward–what I want is the immigration to that country–I am not clairvoyant- but I am gifted in counsulting (sic) with the spirits at an appropriate time–this is away how I have been working. I do not divulge who did anything–because this would endanger my life–I wish to go and live in your country to work the years remaining in my life–I wish to get out of this type of life in Mexico–I can clear other problems that have not been solved in Mexico– I can clear other problems that have not been solved

or found–with anything further I am awaiting your attention. Signed (name redacted by FOIA office).

Mrs. Schrock wrote in an October 6 letter to my successor that she did not take either "psychic" report seriously. In the letter she noted in part that the area near the truck had been thoroughly searched by Michael Oreste, the Mexican army and me, and that she had also walked over it during her July 1982 visit. At the time (July 1982) we reported to her that we had thoroughly searched the area in question and found nothing to indicate a body was buried there. However we also stressed that we were searching a full month after he might have been killed. In the intervening time (from when he disappeared to when we first searched the area) the dry season's lack of rain and high temperatures had baked the soil, making it difficult to find any sign of a month-old burial. In her letter Mrs. Schrock also agreed there was no need to follow up on these "leads." And that was the last of the reports regarding activity in the search for Professor Schrock during 1983.

1984

We had finally reached George Orwell's much feared title year describing a dystopian future. In Mazatlán it was a relatively quiet year, at least in terms of the continued search for Professor Nicholas Wickham Schrock. I was no longer working in Mexico but had transferred to Germany. While I tried to keep up with developments in the case, it was harder in the days before the internet and email. In fact, the State Department was only just beginning to distribute the old Wang desktop word processing desktop computers to the field. My office in Germany, for example, only received two of the units for a staff of 15 officers and other employees, most of whom did not appreciate their utility. As to progress on looking for Professor Schrock, the State Department was only able to provide me a very few documents under my Freedom of Information Act request that covered developments in 1984.

My colleagues who served there at the time were unable to recall any relevant activity during that year other than the continuing ad campaign. The trail had run cold. The State Department's files show only two Congressional requests for information the entire year; one in March by Congress member Mary Rose Oakar and one in June by Dan Schaefer. Both requested a general status update and asked about one of the rumored sightings that had occurred in 1983 and already had been found to be erroneous.

Most of the activities of the Consulates in Guadalajara, Hermosillo and Mazatlán, and of the Embassy in Mexico City involved maintaining contact with Mexican state and federal law enforcement agencies and providing updates. It was clear, however, that while local authorities were on the lookout for any developments regarding Professor Schrock, they were not actively searching for him or investigating his disappearance. The three Consulates continued to be actively engaged in pursuing the radio and newspaper ad campaigns that began in 1983. Radio spots and newspaper ads were run weekly until sometime in May when Mrs. Schrock decided to suspend the effort.

There was one noteworthy development. In early February, the University of Colorado received an unsigned two-page letter typed in Spanish purporting to explain what happened to Professor Schrock. The envelope had no return address and was mailed in Palm Springs, California on February 7. A copy was also purportedly sent to Mrs. Schrock. The University quickly sent their copy to Consul General Larry Lane in Mexico City for further investigation. Most of the letter identifies individuals and companies allegedly involved in drug trafficking in Mexico and will not be included in this narrative. However, the first paragraph refers directly to Professor Schrock and, therefore, the translation by the University of Colorado is included as follows:

> The events I will narrate started in Tijuana Baja California (North) with the assassination of a person nicknamed "El Mano Negra" (the Black Hand). We do not know the motive. After this assassins followed

from Tijuana the footsteps of Mr. Nicholas Wickman (sic) Schrock to the city of Culiacán, Sinaloa, where he lived for a short time. He was kidnapped by the gang of Manuel Salcido Auzeta, alias "El Cochiloco" (Crazy Pig). According to what is known it was because Mr. Schrock was coming to investigate him regarding narcotics traffic – once captured he was tortured to make him talk – later sacrificed and buried secretly in the region of Microhondas Hill, located between Culiacán and El Espinal on the International Highway. After committing this act, they abandoned the truck close to the town of San Ignacio, Sinaloa, where it was used by the authorities there. Cochi said they could keep it.

The letter is interesting but raises a number of questions. There was a drug lord active at the time called Manuel Salcido Auzeta and one of his aliases was indeed "El Cochiloco." I don't know why most Mexican criminals have nicknames or where they get them, but this one is particularly interesting. In any event, he was reportedly very active initially in the Guadalajara cartel and was a co-founder of the Sinaloa cartel. Coincidentally, he was supposedly born in San Ignacio in 1946, a further reason to believe that the San Ignacio area was, as we were told initially, "very dangerous." He was later murdered by Colombian drug dealers in 1991. There is no reason to believe that Professor Schrock had any involvement in any drug activities in Mexico. All the evidence indicates he was exactly what he purported to be, a dedicated professor who disappeared while driving along the InterAmerican Highway.

The letter is questionable for a number of other reasons.

There is no evidence that Professor Schrock was in Tijuana, nor that he spent several days in Culiacán. Believing the bus driver that initially spotted the vehicle, the timing wouldn't work out for more than a night or two in Culiacán. While it is always possible that the Professor was killed in a case of mistaken identity, the timeline does not work out. In addition, El Spinal is a small town about fifteen miles north of Mazatlán and not on the InterAmerican Highway. It is also some distance south toward Mazatlán from where the Professor's pickup was found abandoned. "Microondas" in English means microwaves. There was a microwave tower near where the Culiacán police were searching for "El Pájaro," but the author of the anonymous letter might have heard that from the press or it was a coincidence as there are quite a few such towers along the length of the main highway. In any event, this lead was investigated by the Embassy and other authorities for more than six months and found not to be credible.

The only other interesting development was contained in an unnumbered wire note from Consulate General Guadalajara to the Embassy in Mexico City dated June 4, 1984, that read:

> Morning of May 31 ACS [American Citizen Services] Section FSN [Foreign Service National/Mexican citizen employee of the Consulate] received a telephone call from a man who said he was a doctor and a former student at the Autonoma [a university in Guadalajara] (wouldn't give his name), who had personally been with Dr. Schrock seven months ago in Hermosillo, Sonora. They were traveling together to Mazatlán,

Sinaloa, where they were detained by Federal Police and accused of having drugs. He reported that the federals beat both him and Dr. Schrock. Informant said he and Schrock were together in jail for four days and then separated, and he never saw or heard from Schrock again. The man also said that during the time they were in jail together they were taken outside the city to a place known as Isla del Pescador. The Consulate Employee requested information about the Schrock car. The informant said that he did not remember it well, but the vehicle was a small van and he remembered nothing more about it. He said he had just been released from jail a few days ago and knew of the search for Schrock.

He steadfastly refused to come into the Consulate even when told his name would not be used. The FSN [consulate employee] handling the call finally asked him to come look at our photograph of Schrock. Later in the day a young man, who said he was a friend, came to take the picture out to the doctor, who he said was waiting two blocks from the Consulate. He was told to have the informant call back if he recognized the picture. No call ever came.

Guadalajara notified Mazatlán by telephone, including all the facts, and Mazatlán requested that we inform the Embassy of what had transpired and request guidance on next steps to be taken. Should Mazatlán begin a search of prisons? For info: Mazatlán reports they know nothing of a prison called Isla del Pescador.

The files provided no further reports on this case and there were no further reports or relevant documents on the search for Professor Schrock for the rest of 1984. The consular staff in Mazatlán regularly visited the prisons in their district that included the states of Sinaloa and Nayarit. We would often get information on developments from other prisoners or staff if an American was being held. I also assume the federal authorities did have small private detention areas they used to question suspects, but not hold them for longer terms, but if so, we were not aware of where they were. I also note that until 2019 there was a federal prison island on Isla Marias, off Puerto Vallarta, which was in Mazatlán's consular district and which I visited once. Although the letter only says, "they were taken to a place known as Isla del Pescador," not that it was a jail. Mazatlán was a major port city for commercial and recreational fishing. There were a number of small islands that could have been referred to locally as "Isla del Pescador," although I never heard them referenced as such.

SATURDAY, APRIL 20, 1985 – A BODY FOUND

The files indicate that the first four-and-a-half months of 1985 were fairly quiet in terms of the search for Professor Schrock. There was one letter from the Mexican ministry for foreign relations to Ambassador John Gavin responding to certain questions he had raised regarding the legal proceedings against the seven San Ignacio suspects and indicating the prosecution's case was still open.

Then on Saturday, April 20, a series of rapid and important developments began concerning the Schrock case. According to sworn statements taken by the attorney general's office, early on Saturday morning two brothers had been dropped off near a microwave transmitter along the InterAmerican Highway. They had planned to cut wood for domestic use. At about 8:30 a.m., while crossing a small arroyo (creek or gully), they encountered half-buried human skeletal remains along with a Timex watch, a pair of Converse All-Star tennis shoes, and some shorts. These were scattered over an area of about ten-meter square and included in that area were a skull, five teeth, leg and other bones. The statements described the arroyo as being only a short distance from where Professor Schrock's vehicle had been abandoned near the 59- kilometer marker on the InterAmerican Highway. Recognizing the importance of their discovery, the brothers immediately decided to report it to the local authorities. As they were on foot, it took them until about 6 p.m. before they could reach the small village of Piaxtla de Abajo and get the communal leader there to report their findings. In their written statement for the Attorney General's office, they swore they did not take anything from the site with them and did not disturb the bones.

The same statements indicate that on the following morning, Sunday, April 21, at about 7:30 a.m., the woodcutters returned to the site accompanied by the Commissioner for Piaxtla (a local communal authority), a judge from Coyotitán, and police from San Ignacio. In their statements, the police and judge described the scene essentially the same as the two woodcutters had reported and searched to see if any other remains were in the area. They said that the remains had apparently been buried in a shallow grave on the edge of the arroyo and that recent heavy rains probably had uncovered them. I remember searching in late June 1982 with the Mexican army along a gully on the west of the area where Professor Schrock's truck was found but not finding any evidence of recently disturbed ground. I remember the area along the gully to be extremely wooded with no open spaces. After examining the site, the judge directed the police to gather the remains and take them back to the main police station in San Ignacio. No photos were taken of the site. This was just a few weeks less than three full years from the date Professor Schrock had disappeared.

According to an April 23 cable report from Mexico City to the State Department in Washington:

> Sinaloa state Attorney General Jorge Chavez Castro informed AmConsulate Mazatlán at approximately

4:25 p.m. EST April 22, 1985, that skeletal remains had been discovered in the general area where the vehicle belonging to Professor Nicholas W. Schrock was found by San Ignacio police (near Coyotitán). Partially buried remains were found by woodcutters on the afternoon of April 21 at the site further away from Highway 15 than the location of the truck. Teeth reported to have some dental work.

In response to a request by Chavez Castro, Consulate delivered Schrock dental records to police in Mazatlán for immediate transfer to Culiacán where the remains were apparently now located. Chavez Castro promised to inform Consulate immediately of results of comparison of dental records with remains, possibly as early as evening of April 22.

Another individual who claimed to have talked to policemen who were at scene of recovery of remains informed Consulate that men's undershorts and a watch were also found with remains.

In consultation with supervisory Consul General Lane in Mexico City, it was decided Consulate Mazatlán would immediately attempt to inform Ruth Schrock by phone of available information. Citizens emergency center will also be informed.

According to a sworn statement made on April 22 by a doctor associated with the attorney general's office, sometime on that same day he traveled to the discovery site by the InterAmerican Highway to examine the area. Finding no more remains or evidence, he and some colleagues went to San Ignacio to examine the skeletal remains to see if they would be able to identify them. They appeared to belong to an adult male. They quickly decided that San Ignacio lacked the sufficient technical equipment to fully examine the remains, so they arranged for the attorney general's office to transport the remains that day to Culiacán where a more fully-equipped examination room was available. The attorney general's office later acknowledged the receipt of copies of Professor Schrock's dental records that night.

Mazatlán Vice Consul Douglas Smith called Mrs. Schrock on the evening of April 22 and gave her the information they had received thus far from Attorney General Chavez Castro and cautioned her that no positive identification had been made, but it was possible that these were the remains of her husband. Mrs. Schrock expressed concern that identification be independently verified before any shipment of remains to the United States. My successor, Vice Consul Smith, was an exceptionally intelligent and hardworking officer. He was also very thorough. Given the unreliability of previous identifications by Sinaloa state authorities, he had already discussed the necessity of an independent verification of all information provided by such authorities with U.S. officials at the Embassy in Mexico City. Smith reported Mrs. Schrock seemed satisfied with the steps being taken by the Consulate.

TUESDAY, APRIL 23 – A BODY IDENTIFIED

The Mexican doctors examining the body must have worked into the night because by the following morning they had produced a six-legal-page report detailing the various bones and their conclusions. The Spanish language report, which I carefully reviewed again for this book, itself largely described the size, shape and condition of the various bones but found they were generally consistent with those of Professor Schrock. The dentist, Dr. Z., was the one who identified the skull and jaw as that of the missing .

The attorney general called Vice Consul Smith around 7 a.m. on April 23 and said that the body had been positively identified as that of Professor Schrock. He added that the watch found with the body was a silver Timex, which fits the description of Professor Schrock's watch provided by Mrs. Schrock. Smith then advised Mrs. Schrock about 7:50 a.m. of the attorney general's identification. He reported that she seemed to be taking it fairly well and they both agreed additional steps needed to be taken to verify the findings.

The Consulate in Mazatlán might have been having trouble with its telex machine for outgoing cables, because later that Tuesday, the Embassy in Mexico City reported to Washington that:

Sinaloa state Attorney General Jorge Chavez Castro

informed the Consulate in Mazatlán by telephone early today (April 23) that remains are those of Nicholas Schrock. Identification was based on comparison of dental records. Corroborating factor was the fact that the watch recovered with remains is a Timex, the type of watch Ruth Schrock says her husband usually wore.

Vice Consul Douglas Smith of Mazatlán is traveling by car this morning to Culiacán together with a dentist contracted by the Consulate to make independent identification. Smith will seek additional details including possible cause of death, and written report from state authorities. He will also verify what is being done to identify and detain persons responsible for Schrock's death.

That morning Dr. Marshall Geer of Thunderbird sent a telex directly to the Consulate in Mazatlán reading:

Mrs. Ruth Schrock, wife of our missing professor Nicholas W. Schrock, has informed us of the discovery of a body possibly that of Nicholas Schrock in the vicinity of the discovery of his truck in 1982. In light of (portion redacted by author) ... previous ludicrous misidentification of other body, we urgently request that competent American forensic pathologists be utilized to identify the remains.

That was what the Consulate and Embassy intended. The Consulate had arranged for an experienced local dentist, "Dr. T" from Mazatlán, who was well-known to the Consulate, to accompany Vice Consul Smith to Culiacán to try to verify the identity of the body. This dentist was a paid consultant for the U.S. government. The two, armed with copies of Professor Schrock's dental records and other physical descriptions, then began the long, hot, bumpy ride to Culiacán. Smith reported his experiences in a cable to Washington and Mexico City on April 24:

> Begin Summary. Consulate Mazatlán has every reason to believe that remains discussed in reftels [previous messages from Mexico City] are those of Professor Nicholas W. Schrock. This belief is based upon the opinion of a dentist who accompanied ConOff [Smith] to view the remains and of certain additional physical evidence allegedly recovered with the remains. Mrs. Schrock was notified of this opinion at approximately 5 p.m. EST on 23 April 85. State Attorney General Chavez Castro assured ConOff that the investigation into Professor Schrock's death remains open and that this new evidence will be given every consideration. End Summary.
>
> Consul Douglas R. Smith traveled to Culiacán, Sinaloa, in the company of [Dr. T], a dentist, on April 23 in order to view the alleged remains of Professor Nicholas W. Schrock. Dr. T was contracted by the Consulate in order to make an independent confirmation of the identity of the remains. A Culiacán dentist [Dr. Z] working with the Attorney General's office, had previously identified the remains as those of Professor Schrock.
>
> The Vice Consul and Dr. T were received by Sinaloa Attorney General Jorge Chavez Castro and Jose Luis Tapia who Chavez Castro said was the

individual in charge of the investigation. (It is ConOff's recollection that Tapia was also involved in the original investigation.) The case was discussed generally during which time ConOff stressed the USG's continuing interest in the total resolution of the affair, including the arrest and conviction of the responsible parties. While Chavez Castro submitted that it was his understanding that the remains exhibited little, if any actual evidence of foul play, he agreed that the circumstances of semi-burial and location did not raise the inference of natural causes. He pointed out that the original murder charges against the seven defendants were dropped precisely to preserve a subsequent possibility of prosecution, should Schrock's body be located. He indicated that the state was prepared to prosecute anyone whom the evidence demonstrated to be culpable, including the original defendants. Tapia was, later, a bit more straightforward, maintaining that a properly identified body was virtually all that had been lacking in order to invite a full homicide prosecution of the original defendants. (As of the morning of April 24, no one has been detained in the matter.)

ConOff and Dr. T were then escorted to a basement room where the non-articulated skeleton and various other items found with it were made available for inspection. The lower jaw of the skeleton contained all the teeth. The dental work corresponded exactly with the dental X-rays provided previously by Mrs. Schrock, according to Dr. T. The upper jaw contained only some five teeth, all molars. The dental work in these also correspond to the X-rays; however, there exists a minor discrepancy between a pictorial dental chart, also supplied by Mrs. Schrock, and the skeleton's dental work. One of the upper molars, charted as containing both gold and silver work, only contains silver.

Aside from this minor discrepancy, Dr. T indicated that all other dental work corresponds to the dental work indicated by the X-rays and chart to be that of Nicholas W. Schrock. Beyond this, the jaw seems to fit perfectly to the rest of the cranium, the bit formed by the teeth when the jaw is closed is virtually perfect, the "median line" (the center of the lower and upper jaw) is perfectly aligned, and Dr. T. indicated that she could determine from the kratom the aftereffects of root surgery on a particular tooth, as is noted on the dental chart.

Apart from the dental coincidences, various other items of physical evidence point to the fact that these are the remains of Professor Schrock. A silver-colored Timex watch with a silver-colored metal Seiko wristband, two "Converse All-Star" tennis shoes, and two red plastic arch supports were allegedly found near the bones. When ConOff telephoned Mrs. Schrock to relay the particulars of the evidence, she confirmed that Schrock wore a similar watch and similar arch supports and that it was highly possible that he had similar tennis shoes.

ConOff took photographs of the remains and the other physical evidence. Dr. T made a formal sworn written statement to the effect that she believes the remains to be those of Professor Schrock. Dr. T stated that the enamel of the front teeth on the lower jaw is cracked. She offered that this is usually indicative of a sharp blow. What is probably the right femur is fractured. A doctor present for much of our examination stated that it was impossible to tell whether or not the fracture occurred before or after the death. It may be possible for U.S. forensic technicians to determine time of fracture. Aside from these two points, neither ConOff nor Dr. T saw any obvious evidence of foul play, although neither is trained for such a determination.

Mrs. Schrock indicated satisfaction with steps taken thus far. She indicated that she wishes the remains forwarded to her, and that she intends to have a complete forensic examination performed on them. She also requested soil samples from the area in which the remains were found. Furthermore, she asserted her interest in seeing the responsible parties brought to justice. ConOff assured Mrs. Schrock that this interest was coincident with that of the USG. Mazatlán will follow up on specific requests. (Drafted by Douglas R. Smith).

WEDNESDAY, APRIL 24 TO TUESDAY, MAY 21 - A THOROUGH EXAMINATION

According to his subsequent report dated May 6, 1985, upon his examination in the United States of the remains identified as Professor Schrock, Dr. X said he first received a telephone call from Mrs. Schrock on the evening of Wednesday April 24. She inquired as to whether Dr. X would examine the skeletal remains presumed to be those of her missing husband. Those remains had been recently recovered from the state of Sinaloa. Although they had been identified by a Mexican dentist as Professor Schrock, she wanted to have an outside confirmation of the identification plus an additional forensic anthropological examination of the skeletal remains to ascertain possible cause of death or indication of perimortem trauma or injury. Mrs. Schrock also wanted to see if there was any evidence the body had been buried or located in more than one place over the three-year period, as well as whether there was any indication of deposition in a saltwater environment at any time. Dr. X agreed to conduct the examination. In that and subsequent conversations, he also agreed on a forensic odontologist to complete the dental portion of the exam.

On Thursday, April 25, the civil registry in Culiacán issued a death certificate for Nicolas (sic) Wickham Schrock, although the Consulate in Mazatlán did not secure a copy until the following evening. The certificate stated the Professor had died sometime in the month of June 1982 near Las Bateas in the municipal area of San Ignacio, Sinaloa, near the 59-kilometer marker in the Nogales-to-Mexico City highway. The cause of death was listed as unknown.

That evening at about 8 p.m., Vice Consul Smith spoke with Attorney General Chavez Castro who said the remains were now at the Consulate's disposal. Chavez Castro suggested that the remains would be brought to the Consulate in Mazatlán at around 2 p.m. Friday, April 26 by Jose Luis Tapia, the prosecutor responsible for investigating the disappearance of Professor Schrock. The attorney general then said Tapia would accompany Smith to view the site where the remains were recovered.

Based on this conversation, Smith thought they might be able to ship the remains on the 2 p.m. Frontier flight to Denver on April 27. Mexicana Airlines no longer carried air freight on its Denver flight. Mrs. Schrock said she would meet the flight at the airport and then transport the remains to Colorado Springs where they would be examined by a physician anthropologist she had selected. She also said that should the remains not be ready for shipment on Saturday, the shipment should be delayed until Tuesday so she could meet it.

On Thursday Vice Consul Smith was informed by Representative Wirth's office that Jesus Michel Jacobo, the defense attorney for six of the seven suspects convicted of theft or improper use of their official powers, had told the press that the San Ignacio police were "digging up bodies" at the site where Professor Schrock's remains were found.

Smith confirmed with a Denver reporter who had been at the site all that day that no such activity was taking place at least until midafternoon.

Late on Friday, April 26, Jose Luis Tapia, an agent of the state district attorney assigned to the State Judicial Police and one of the prosecutors to investigate the case, arrived at the Consulate in Mazatlán. Tapia brought the human remains believed to be those of Nicholas Schrock along with a copy of the death certificate and a copy of the report by a medical-legal expert (medico legista), which recited a detailed analysis of the recovered bones and concluded they were of a white male, roughly 1.7 meters tall and between 40 and 45 years old. The remains did not yield sufficient information to determine a cause of death.

The remains were packed in plastic bags and placed in a receptacle supplied by a local Mazatlán funeral home. They were later sealed by an employee of the funeral home on the consular premises and given to the custody of the funeral home for crating and forwarding to Mrs. Schrock. Tapia had not brought the transit permit with him from Culiacán; thus, the remains could not be shipped the next day. Therefore, in compliance with Mrs. Schrock's wishes, the remains would not be forwarded before Tuesday, April 30.

As it was far too late to view the site where the remains were found, Tapia and Smith held a lengthy conversation on the case. Tapia said off-the-record that the state police were currently searching for at least three of the original seven suspects. He also gave Smith a copy of an order from the state director of investigations (Director de Averiguaciones Previas) to the director of the State Judicial Police that he clarify the facts of the case through further investigation.

On Monday, April 29, Mazatlán Vice Consul Douglas Smith and prosecutor Jose Luis Tapia traveled to the site where the remains of Professor Schrock were said to be found. Smith later reported:

> The site was 59 kilometers north of Mazatlán (8 kilometers south of the gasoline station at Coyotitán where Schrock was last seen by anyone other than his presumed murderers), immediately south of a series of curves known commonly as Las Bateas. A dirt road, allegedly used by woodcutters, heads east off Highway 15 and eventually winds its way to the top of a hill where Professor Schrock's truck was located under an electrical transmission tower. Approximately one hundred yards down the western slope of the hill (as the crow flies), ten to fifteen meters off a branch of the same dirt road, lies the area where the remains were found. The majority of the bones, including the cranium, jawbone, and larger leg bones, were located along the shoulders of a small wash which cuts steeply through the area. Bones were found on each side of this wash. It would appear that it carries substantial amounts of water during the rainy season. The shoulders are much wider, flatter areas. The entire area is covered with thick brush and small trees. ConOff [Smith] took roughly twelve photos of the area in general and two soil samples, which will be forwarded to Mrs. Schrock pursuant to her request."

Vice Consul Smith reported that information to Mrs. Schrock later that day, and also confirmed the shipping arrangements for the remains the following day. The soil samples were requested to try to verify whether the soil in the area matched that found on the remains to see if the body had been reburied at any point.

On Tuesday, April 30, the remains of Professor Schrock were transported to Denver on the afternoon Frontier Airlines flight. The permission to transport from the Mexican government had arrived at the Consulate on the afternoon of April 29. The University of Colorado Foundation paid for the shipment with money transferred through the State Department to the Mazatlán Consulate. The remains themselves were contained in a sealed child's coffin. Along with the remains, the Consulate shipped five X-rays (two of the feet, two of the lumbar spine, and two dental sets) and a notarized consular mortuary certificate.

On arrival in Denver, Mrs. Schrock and some family members accepted the shipment and transported the remains to Colorado Springs where they were accepted by Dr. X and his colleagues. In his May 6 written report, Dr. X noted:

> The remains were received in a gray, child's coffin which was seated on a wooden pallet, over which was a heavy corrugated cardboard box tied with manila twine. In addition to the shipping label the box indicated "Human Remains." The coffin lid was sealed with a clear silicone sealant. Opening the coffin revealed a white satin-lined interior filled with skeletal material enclosed in twelve semi-transparent plastic bags. Other plastic bags were wadded up and used as fill-in packing material. Initial inspection revealed little or no breakage of material as a result of transport

from Mexico.

The remainder of the evening of April 30 was spent removing the contents of each plastic bag and doing a quick inventory of material present. This initial inventory revealed a rather clean, nearly complete, non-fragmented, human adult male skeleton whose general characteristics fit those of Professor Schrock. There was not a trace of soft tissue present and only minimal amounts of adherent soil, the latter being either a loosely adherent dark-brown humus with some leafy fragments present or a strongly adherent pinkish-red clay-like material. Most bones showed evidence of surface weathering, i.e., bleaching to a light gray color with fine surficial cracking; minimal carnivore tooth marks and evidence of chewing were present. There was no odor to any of the material."

The doctor also noted the six X-rays and other material delivered by Mrs. Schrock and in her presence signed an evidence transfer form.

The following morning, Wednesday, May 1, Dr. X and his colleagues began their careful examination of the remains. As the report is quite lengthy and technical, I will summarize some of the findings. The skeleton was consistent with the physical characteristics of Professor Schrock in that it was of a Caucasian male, approximately 39-44 years at the time of death and roughly 5 feet, 7 inches to 5 feet, 11 inches tall. He also noted that "all the skeletal remains "fit together very well" and are consistent with the remains of one individual.

As to the cause of death, there was femoral fracture,

but insufficient evidence to state whether it occurred before or shortly after death. He noted that "usually the result of rather strong forces on the bone such as one typically sees in automobile and motorcycle accidents. The lack of other signs of injury or trauma on the remainder of the skeleton, particularly the head and chest, lessens the argument that the broken femur is the result of a bludgeoning or the result of the body being thrown down into an arroyo or gully."

The examination of the skull, jaw and teeth showed little evidence to support significant trauma to the head or death. Any damage could be explained by normal pre- or post-mortem processes. In addition, there was:

> no evidence of knife or gunshot wounds, or general blunt trauma; again, especially in the head and chest region. In fact, other than the femoral fracture, the skeleton is in remarkably complete and intact condition. Other injuries are consistent with known prior injuries or processes in an athletic adult male.

Dr. X also looked at the question of where the body was found and whether it had been moved. He said the weathering of the bones suggested they had been on the ground surface for probably at least a year. The minimal amount of animal tooth marks and chewing suggested the body was buried for a year or two before it was uncovered. The spread over an area was consistent with water washing and animal moving. His overall impression was that the body was buried at the site and erosion scattered it over the ground surface. There was nothing to indicate the body had been moved, or at least not moved in the last two to three years.

On the evening of Wednesday May 1, the skull, jaw and teeth were examined by a forensic odontologist. After a thorough examination of the items and comparison with known records for Professor Schrock, both the forensic odontologist and Dr. X opined the comparisons were compatible and that all apparent discrepancies were explainable. This led them to make a positive identification that the remains were those of Professor Nicholas Wickham Schrock.

In early May Mrs. Schrock suggested to Vice Consul Smith that now that they had identified her husband her occasional questions and remarks were less urgent, so she suggested they use written correspondence rather than talking on the telephone. I imagine she was probably fatigued with three years of hearing the phone ring, wondering what news it might bring and yet having to pick up the receiver. She was still determined to find out what happened to her husband and to push the Mexican authorities to find and punish those responsible, as were the consular staff in Mazatlán.

Most of the early correspondence between Mrs. Schrock and Vice Consul Smith centered around providing additional information to Dr. X and his team regarding the site where the remains were discovered and whether there were any photos taken by Mexican authorities when they first found the site. It appears there were not. During May Vice Consul Smith also sent Mrs. Schrock the shoes, arch supports, undershorts and watch that were found with the body along with photos he had taken on April 29 when he visited the site. When she received them, Mrs. Schrock noted that everything looked familiar as probably belonging to her husband. She noted, however, that the watch band (a Seiko on a Timex watch) was unfamiliar, but since he had been teaching in Japan prior to his entry into Mexico, he might have needed to replace the band in Japan. Smith also provided her with a Report of the Death of an American Citizen Abroad, which she would need as evidence of death for various legal matters. It noted the date and cause of death were "not determined by local authorities."

In their correspondence, Mrs. Schrock mentioned the possibility of returning to Mazatlán to visit the site where the body was discovered. Later that fall she appears to have decided not to make the trip, at least not in 1985.

WEDNESDAY, MAY 22 THROUGH DECEMBER

As the remains of Professor Schrock had been identified and shipped to the United States, the focus in the case was gradually shifting back to efforts to push the Mexican law enforcement agencies to invigorate their investigation of what happened to the professor and who was responsible. In a letter dated May 22, 1985, to Mrs. Schrock, Vice Consul Doug Smith wrote:

> Lic. Tapia informed me that the State Judicial Police are currently actively searching for all seven individuals previously implicated in your husband's death. To date there have been no arrests. Lic. Tapia offered that two of the individuals sought still maintain residences in San Ignacio, but that they have (allegedly) not been seen since shortly after news of the recovery of the remains was broken. He added that most believe them to have fled into the surrounding mountains. Lic. Tapia is expecting a report from the Director of the State Judicial Police, Lic. Roberto Robles Rendon, pursuant to the request made by the state director of pending investigations. He has promised to inform me of the contents of the report and of any additional significant developments. I expect to meet with him privately early next week.

With regard to the site where the remains were discovered, Lic. Tapia informed me that some of the bones were completely above ground when they were recovered and that others were partially buried. He emphasized that none was completely buried. No photographs were taken.

There was also some back and forth regarding the collection of the soil over the next few weeks such as location and depth. Vice Consul Smith noted he was going to leave Mazatlán in mid-August as a part of a routine transfer. Mrs. Schrock wrote that she really appreciated all the work that Smith had done regarding the finding, repatriation of remains, and continuing investigation in her husband's case. As to the investigation, on June 17, 1985, Vice Consul Smith wrote that he had spoken with Tapia again on June 16. The Embassy had apparently heard a rumor that there had been three arrests in connection with Professor Schrock's murder. The rumor proved to be false as Tapia denied that any arrests had been made. Smith wrote there was also a rumor that at least one of the suspects had been seen in Culiacán, but again said that appeared to be just a rumor.

On Tuesday, August 6, in what looks to be the last letter Vice Consul Smith wrote to Mrs. Schrock before being transferred, Smith said that he had been able to talk to one of the two brothers "who were credited with discovery of your husband's remains." Smith wrote that the brother seemed a credible and straightforward witness who answered all his questions. He noted that while it was only his opinion, he did not believe the brother was "party to any moving of the remains, if indeed the remains had been moved before he stumbled upon them." He also added:

> There have still been no arrests in the case although authorities continue to insist that they are searching for the previous defendants. We may be able to make use of a new federal office designed to assist state authorities in cases of crimes against American citizens, should this inability to locate these suspects continue.

On August 14 the final soil analysis report was released. This supplemented a longer report completed on May 26. The second report had taken longer than normal because of the small size of the sample collected from the remains. This meant several tests used routinely could not be utilized and more sophisticated and extensive methods were undertaken. The experts used X-ray diffraction analysis on the samples instead of trace element analysis as originally considered. The author of the principal study wrote:

> From the soil analyses I conclude:
>
> 1. The soil sample taken from the skeleton (1) is basically the same as the sample taken near the skeleton (3). There is no evidence of any soil from another location being found on the skeleton.
>
> 2. The soil sample taken from upstream (2) was somewhat different from the other two. This was suspected from initial visual analysis and is only logical because of the alleged method of collection.
>
> 3. Samples 2 and 3 were somewhat different from each other, therefore if sample 1 were very similar to

either of these samples, there would be no evidence of the skeleton being moved.

On August 30 Mrs. Schrock began her correspondence with Vice Consul Steven Toy who replaced Doug Smith at the Consulate in Mazatlán. She again praised Smith for the work he had done and asked Toy to feel free to call her anytime there was a development he judged sufficiently important to telephone. Otherwise, Mrs. Schrock wrote she was satisfied with written updates and responses to her questions.

According to a cable sent October 3, on Tuesday, September 17 a consular officer from Mazatlán, probably Vice Consul Toy:

> called the San Ignacio District Attorney's Office to speak with Mr. Tapia, the individual who had been heading the investigation (into the disappearance of Professor Schrock), in order to request the averiguacion previa number from the initial investigatory document of mid-1982. A new district attorney, Lic. Luis Gerardo Perez Benitez, stated that Mr. Tapia had been removed from the investigation, and that he no longer worked for the District Attorney's Office. The DA would state neither why nor when Mr. Tapia was removed from the case and added that all the records in the case had been sent to the Attorney General's office in Culiacán. The new Sinaloa Attorney General, Gilberto Zazueta Felix, had taken charge of the case.

This was a fairly dramatic series of personnel changes in terms of the ongoing search for those responsible for the death of Professor Schrock. Vice Consul Toy was able to reach the new attorney general, Gilberto Zazueta Felix, on Wednesday, September 18 to discuss the case. During that conversation the attorney general confirmed that he was personally in charge of the case and said that individuals were actively being sought. He also said the preliminary investigation document (averiguacion previa) was open, and that there were no specific charges included at the time. He added that investigators would need to question suspects before the specific charges could be added. Toy asked for a copy of the preliminary investigation document.

On Monday, September 23, Mazatlán Vice Consul Toy again called the attorney general in Culiacán to press for a written update on the case as well as any investigatory documents. The attorney general said he would send copies of the latest results. In response to questioning from Toy regarding the identity of the suspects being investigated, the attorney general replied, "...that the initial seven suspects had been cleared of all charges in connection with the case and offered no explanation as to when the seven were cleared or why." This was also a major development in the case since the former attorney general, in his recent communications, had indicated that the investigators were searching for the original seven suspects.

On Thursday, September 26, after receiving some documents from Culiacán, Vice Consul Toy again called the attorney general. While thanking him for sending him the documents, Toy noted it was a copy of the study of the skeletal remains found in April that the Consulate already possessed rather than the prosecutorial documents from 1982 and the most recent investigation, which Toy had requested. The attorney general said there had never been an averiguacion previa or formal investigation document opened in mid-1982 when the seven original suspects had been charged but promised to send other prosecution documents.

On Friday, September 27, Vice Consul Toy wrote his first status update letter to Mrs. Schrock who had written to him on August 30. He apologized for the late response, but said he wanted to have a firm grip on the facts of the case, including reviewing the file and talking to Mexican law enforcement officials, before contacting her. He also noted that in addition to the departure of Vice Consul Smith, the other vice consul, "an excellent officer," who had not yet been replaced meant the Consulate was shorthanded. He regretted that he had little new information to report regarding the investigation. He briefed her on the changes in Mexican prosecutorial personnel and the fact the seven initial suspects continue to be free on all charges. He also noted that the new attorney general had been vague in terms of who his office was investigating or what specific steps they had taken.

On Monday, September 30, Vice Consul Toy called the office of the district attorney in San Ignacio. He first spoke to the secretary to the district attorney and then to one of the prosecutors. Both indicated that all documents regarding the Schrock case had been transferred to authorities in Culiacán and the San Ignacio office was not directly involved in the continuing investigations. Toy then called and spoke with the new attorney general for the fourth time that month. Toy thanked the attorney general for sending some additional documents, but noted they were copies of testimony from the two individuals that claimed to have found the body, which the Consulate had previously received. The attorney general responded that copies of all investigation documents from 1982 onwards had already been sent to various consular officers in Mazatlán. Toy reported his conversations with the attorney general by telephone to Department officials in Washington and with Embassy officials. He also noted the complete lack of progress in getting current and responsive information from the attorney general and requested the Embassy directly contact the attorney general. In other words, the new attorney general in Sinaloa was no longer cooperating with the Consulate.

On Friday, October 4, Mazatlán Vice Consul Steven Toy wrote a detailed letter to Sinaloa state Attorney General Zazueta Felix in Culiacán requesting specific documents that he had also requested in his telephone calls. He also asked for a comprehensive status update of the efforts by the law enforcement officials of the state of Sinaloa to investigate the disappearance/murder of Professor Schrock. He sent copies to the relevant Mexican officials in San Ignacio and Culiacán as well as to the supervisory Consul General in the U.S. Embassy in Mexico City. In a follow up letter on Tuesday, November 26, Toy again requested the attorney general provide a status report on the Schrock investigation as well as information regarding the investigations of several crimes against U.S. citizens that took place in 1984 and 1985. There is no evidence the attorney general ever responded.

1986

Developments began slowly in 1986 regarding the search to discover what happened to Professor Nicholas Schrock in late May or early June 1982. A good portion of the bureaucratic efforts in the case during 1986 focused on untangling financial records related to the various search ad campaigns undertaken in 1982, 1983, and 1984. In one letter written by Vice Consul Toy to Mrs. Schrock complaining about the difficulty in untangling these accounts, Toy noted:

> "There appears to have been more attention paid to the investigation itself than to the procurement of copies of checks and receipts, on the part of the Consulate."

The issue was also complicated by the fact that during the 1981 to 1984 period, the Mexican economy was collapsing so that the exchange rate was in constant decline. This meant that the funds provided in dollars that were converted into pesos over time at drastically different exchange rates and expended in pesos, with perhaps less than desirable recordkeeping. It was not until the end of October 1986 that Mrs. Schrock, the University of Colorado Foundation, the Consulates in Hermosillo, Guadalajara and Mazatlán, and -- perhaps most importantly -- the

State Department in Washington all agreed on the final accounting. A trivial, but very time-consuming matter.

The principal focus during 1986 however remained the encouragement of Mexican law enforcement authorities to reinvigorate their efforts in investigating what happened to Professor Schrock. This was not a successful endeavor. In the words of Vice Consul Toy responding on March 14, 1986, to a January 29 letter from Mrs. Schrock:

Since I last corresponded with you on September 27, 1985, there have been *no developments at all in the investigation* (emphasis added by author). I hasten to add that I have written the Attorney General, Lic. Gilberto Zazueta Felix, on two separate occasions. Mr. Zazueta Felix has failed to respond to any of these requests for a full investigation that would bring the case to a close.

In a March 13 cable to the Embassy in Mexico City largely focused on other matters, the Consulate in Mazatlán notes that the Sinaloa attorney general has failed to answer any and all correspondence regarding the Schrock case since October 1985. Other letters and copies of the correspondence to the attorney general sent to other law enforcement officials in San Ignacio and Culiacán had similarly not received any responses. On Tuesday, March 18, Toy sent yet another letter to Attorney General Gilberto Zazueta Felix regarding a status report on the Schrock investigation. That letter was also never answered. On Monday, March 31, the Embassy requested a copy of all the letters from Toy to the attorney general so that the Embassy could follow up at higher levels. Toy forwarded the documents later that week, noting the attorney general had also been unresponsive to requests involving crimes against other U.S. citizens in

Sinaloa.

While the next developments in the Schrock case may or may not have been due to complaints or actions by the U.S. Embassy in Mexico City, they did further complicate efforts to discover what had happened to Professor Schrock. In an April 22 letter from Vice Consul Toy to Mrs. Schrock he wrote:

> Current political changes in Sinaloa will have an effect, though not necessarily a positive one, on the way investigations will be conducted here for some time to come. Within the last two weeks, the Attorney General of Sinaloa, Gilberto Zazueta Felix, and the Director of the Sinaloa Judicial Police, Mr. Robles Rendon, have both resigned. The new Attorney General of Sinaloa, Jose Roberto Camacho Castro, very probably will know little about the case, but I shall be familiarizing him with it shortly.
>
> I have sent copies of the letters that had been mailed to the former Attorney General to the U.S. Embassy in Mexico City. Officers there will be protesting the lack of action with the Secretariat of Foreign Relations.

Vice Consul Toy was right. The resignations of the attorney general and state head of investigations did not bode well for further vigorous investigations in the Schrock case, at least not in the short run. On Friday April 25, 1986, the U.S. Embassy in Mexico City delivered the following diplomatic note to the Government of Mexico:

No. 745

The Embassy of the United States of America presents its compliments to the Ministry of Foreign Affairs and has the honor to bring to the attention of the Ministry the murder case of Nicholas Schrock.

Nicholas Schrock was reported missing in June 1982. On June 28, 1982, officials of the United States Consulate in Mazatlán found his vehicle and its contents at the San Ignacio police station. Schrock's remains were not found and identified until April 1985, after which Averiguacion Previa number 19/895 was assigned to the case. On July 15, 1985, (Proceso No. 83/982), the defendants were found guilty of theft and dereliction of duty.

In four separate phone calls to Sinaloa Attorney General Gilberto Zazueta Felix in September 1985, the Consul was given conflicting information about the existence and location of the 1982 Averiguacion Previa. On October 4, 1985, the Consulate sent a letter to Licenciado Gilberto Zazueta Felix requesting the original averiguación previa of 1982. On November 26, 1985, the Consulate again wrote to Licenciado Gilberto Zazueta Felix inquiring as to the progress in the investigation. On March 18, 1986, another letter was sent. None of the correspondence since October 1985 has been answered.

The Embassy is deeply concerned over the lack of response to the correspondence concerning Mr. Schrock. The Embassy requests the Ministry's assistance in obtaining information on the status of Averiguacion Previa No. 19/985.

The Embassy of the United States of America avails itself of this opportunity to renew the Secretariat of Foreign Relations of the United Mexican States its assurances of its highest consideration.

Embassy of the United States of American

Mexico, D.F., April 25, 1986

During July 1983 when the prosecution rested in the case against the seven San Ignacio policemen, then-Attorney General Jorge Chavez Castro told me the reason the charges of homicide had been dropped was because no body had been found and most of the seven had recanted their confessions. He also stated that by dropping the charges, the prosecution could then recharge them should Professor Schrock's body be found. Since the body of the Professor had been recovered, in April 1986, U.S. officials in Washington, Mexico City and Mazatlán renewed an effort to press for the rearrest of the police officials responsible. The Consulate in Mazatlán reported in a July 25, 1986 cable to Mexico City that:

Neither of the two more recent Sinaloa Attorneys General has made any effort to recharge any of the initial seven defendants with homicide. In May 1986, ConOff [probably Vice Consul Steven Toy] presented circuit delegate Angel Saad Said with copies of the court documents that indicated the reasons for the initial release of the defendants, and that indicated that Schrock's remains had in fact been found. Saad noted the extraordinarily poor quality of the release warrant and stated to ConOff that he would see whether he could justify federal intervention into the case in order to have it reopened. On June 23, 1986, ConOff presented copies of the same court documents to Culiacán District Attorney Evariso E. Perez Villareal, and requested that he present the documents to the current Sinaloa Attorney General Camacho Castro for study. To date Camacho Castro, like Saad Said, has not responded to ConOff's requests that the trial be reopened. On July 23, ConOff again requested that the AG reopen the case.

On Thursday July 31, Mazatlán Vice Consul Toy wrote the new Sinaloa Attorney General Jose Roberto Camacho Castro a letter again requesting clarification of the status of the investigation and whether any of the original defendants initially charged with homicide would be reindicted, since the remains of Professor Schrock had been found and identified. Toy met with Camacho Castro the following day, Friday, August 1, for one and a half hours to discuss the Schrock case and other similar matters. The attorney general was accompanied by Sinaloa Judicial Police Director Bernardo Riveros Acosta. Toy was right when he wrote to Mrs. Schrock on April 22nd saying:

> The new Attorney General of Sinaloa, Jose Roberto Camacho Castro, very probably will know little about the case, but I shall be familiarizing him with it shortly.

In his cabled report of the meeting, Toy indicated neither the attorney general nor the director were aware that the remains of Professor Schrock had been found in

April 1985. They also were unaware that the case was still open, and that murder charges could (according to the court documents) still be filed against the initial seven defendants. The Attorney General reportedly stated that he had not read the file but would do so to see whether the seven defendants might again be charged. It is interesting that there is a push by U.S. officials to reindict all seven suspects since only a few had been originally charged with homicide. Toy subsequently noted that he also raised the issue of reindictment as well as the need for a reinvigorated investigation in meetings with agents of the Mexican Attorney General's office at the Consulate in Mazatlán on August 6.

During 1986 there were also changes in personnel in Mexico City. After five years, on June 10, 1986, Ambassador John Gavin ended his time in Mexico and returned to the United States to work in the private sector. His successor, Ambassador Charles J. Pilliod Jr., did not arrive in Mexico until November 4, 1986.

In a letter to Vice Consul Toy on August 19, Mrs. Schrock raised the idea of setting up a small fund to help other Americans searching for friends and relatives in Mexico. Along with rising drug trafficking and violence in Mexico in general in the second half of the 1980s, there were an increasing number of criminal incidents directed at U.S. citizens. Toy responded on September 15 that he thought it was a useful suggestion and that day also wrote acting Consul General in Mexico City, Richard Peterson, passing along the idea for consideration. I found no other mention of the fund in the files I received following my 1989 Freedom of Information Act request.

There continued to be an apparent complete lack of progress in the Schrock investigation by Mexican law enforcement officials throughout the rest of 1986. In a cabled report to Washington on October 21 the Consulate in Mazatlán wrote:

Despite a lengthy discussion of the Schrock case during the meetings between ConOff and the Sinaloa Attorney General on August 1, 1986, no investigation progress appears to have been made. Post notes that the summary of this case provided by Federal Attorney General Representative Jose Maria Ortega Padilla to EmbOffs on September 12, 1986, misconstrued the facts regarding the finding of Schrock's remains. According to the erroneous summary, Schrock's supposed remains were located in April 1985, and then found to be those of some other individual once they were shipped to the U.S. In fact, two sets of remains have been found, the first of which was found in 1983 and determined to be those of someone else, and the latter which was found in April 1985 and determined by both Mexican authorities and U.S. forensic experts to be definitely those of Schrock. Moreover, the summary does not address the point of whether the initial seven defendants can be once again tried for the murder of Schrock. The trial record clearly indicates that the murder charge was dismissed because no body could be found, rather than the defendants were found innocent of the charges. Beyond that, post records indicate that then-Sinaloa Attorney General Chavez Castro stated to a Mazatlán ConOff that the murder charge was being dropped specifically so that were the remains ever to be found, the individual could be recharged with the crime.

Vice Consul Toy followed up with a letter on Wednesday,

October 22, to Sinaloa Attorney General Jose Roberto Camacho Castro again asking for prosecution documents and an update on the investigation into the murder of Professor Schrock. There is no indication that that letter was ever answered.

On December 12 Vice Consul Toy wrote his last letter to Mrs. Schrock in which he informed her that he would be leaving the Consulate (routine transfer) by the end of the year. He also reported at least some progress in getting Mexican federal officials involved in the investigation. His was not to be the only departure at the end of that year. On December 31, 1986, the six-year term of Sinaloa Governor Antonio Toledo Corro ended. Mexican governors can only serve one term.

THE REWARD

And what of the $5,000 reward for information leading to the discovery of Professor Schrock? On July 3, 1985, Mazatlán Vice Consul Douglas Smith wrote Mrs. Schrock that he was trying to get contact information from the San Ignacio prosecutor for the two brothers that had allegedly located the remains of Professor Schrock. Smith understood the brothers were interested in any available reward. He added that he assumed she would support an effort to process an award for them should it appear that they had no involvement in the case other than finding the remains. Smith interviewed one of the brothers who openly and at length responded to his questions regarding the events leading up to their discovery of the remains and their subsequent actions in reporting the findings. Smith found him credible and prepared an affidavit that was completed by one of the brothers. One of these affidavits read:

"Before me, the undersigned authority, on this day personally appeared (name redacted by author), of Culiacán, Sinaloa, Mexico, who after first being by me duly sworn placed under oath stated as follows:

"My name is (name redacted by author). I reside in Culiacán, Sinaloa. I visit my parents, who live near San Ignacio, Sinaloa on a regular basis, usually every weekend. On one of these visits, on 20 April 1985, I went with my brother (name also redacted), to cut some wood in an area near Las Bateas, Sinaloa. While we were cutting some wood, we discovered what appeared to be human remains. We notified the head of the local communal farm, who in turn informed the responsible authorities of the discovery. As later events proved, these remains were the remains of Professor Nicholas W. Schrock. Because my discovery was instrumental in determining the whereabouts of Professor Schrock, I feel that I am entitled to the reward offered by the University of Colorado, and I hereby request the same. I intend to share the reward with my brother (name redacted). This statement was translated to me in Spanish, and I understand it completely before signing it."

The affidavit was witnessed by Vice Consul Smith on July 8. He then forwarded it, along with supporting documents signed by the State Director for Investigations, Gilberto Zazuela Felix, and the San Ignacio prosecutor, Pedro Tirado Iribe, to officials at the University of Colorado for action. Vice Consul Smith was then routinely transferred from Mazatlán and left post in the second week of August.

The general counsel to the University of Colorado wrote back to Smith in a letter dated September 3, 1985. In it he had a number of questions regarding the request for the reward. He wanted to have more information regarding the two brothers, more background facts regarding the discovery of the remains and more details regarding how Smith came into contact with the brothers. Finally, the general counsel wanted to know that should the University decide to pay the brothers the reward whether the Consulate would assist in its payment. Unfortunately, since Smith had departed post, the letter was either misdirected or never arrived at the Consulate. (It was sent through international mail through the Mexican postal system rather than to the Consulate's letter drop in Laredo, Mexico.) Neither the Consulate nor the University took any further action during 1985 to follow up on the request for a reward.

In a Wednesday, January 29, 1986, letter to Vice Consul Toy by Mrs. Schrock asking for a status update on the investigation, she also questioned if he knew whether the University of Colorado had ever paid a reward for those who found her husband's skeleton. On Friday, March 14, Vice Consul Toy wrote a letter to Mrs. Schrock in which he stated that the Consulate had no record as to whether the two brothers had sent their depositions and requests to claim the reward. The Consulate did have copies of the affidavits, but no cover letter or anything to indicate they were sent. He also sent a letter to the University of Colorado Foundation stating Mrs. Schrock was asking whether the Foundation had paid the $5,000 dollar reward. In that letter he offered to send the affidavit and supporting documents to the Foundation if they had not already received them. He speculated that perhaps the Foundation never received the formal request. He also noted the brothers had called the Consulate numerous times asking if the Foundation had made a decision. (Yet the Consulate did not follow up until Mrs. Schrock raised the issue).

On Tuesday, April 1, 1986, the general counsel of the University of Colorado answered Vice Consul Toy's letter. He sent along a copy of his September 3, 1985, letter and indicated he had never received any response. He still needed the basic questions raised in the letter answered in order to help him "wrap up matters on this end." He ended by stating, "If this information could be provided to the University it would thereafter be in a better position to make a decision."

On Tuesday, May 20, 1986, Vice Consul Toy wrote to the University's general counsel, with a copy to Mrs. Schrock, first noting that the Consulate had never received his letter of September 3 and that Vice Consul Smith, who handled the matter had left post. He then admitted that he was not "well-enough versed" with Smith's knowledge of the circumstances surrounding the finding of the remains and thus was not in a position to answer the first three questions posed in the original letter. He then added that he had contacted Smith who said he was readily agreeable to answering the general counsel's questions.

On Monday, July 28, the general counsel of the University of Colorado wrote to then acting Principal Officer Toy with a copy to Mrs. Schrock. He said that after receiving the May 20 letter he had heard from Douglas Smith. Based on his discussion with Smith, "a determination has been made to pay the reward amount to [the brothers]." He then asked again whether the Consulate could assist in facilitating the payment and provide a contact point to handle the details. "Your prompt reply would be appreciated by all."

Slowly but surely, the process continued. On Tuesday, September 9, the Principal Officer in Mazatlán wrote the contact at the University of Colorado, acknowledging the July 28 letter, saying, "This Consulate would be pleased to act as an intermediary of the purposes of a transfer of the funds." More than four months later, on Wednesday, January

21, 1987, a vice consul in Mazatlán wrote to the brothers to inform them that the Consulate had received their reward check and requested they contact the Consulate to receive it. The final item is a letter dated Wednesday, February 4, 1987, to the contact point at the University of Colorado informing them that the reward check for assistance in discovering the remains of Professor Schrock was presented to the brothers on January 29. It added that at the request of the brothers, the Consulate did not publicize the event. The letter enclosed a copy of the receipt.

THE FINAL DEVELOPMENTS

On January 14, 1987, the State Department notified the Consulate in Mazatlán that Mrs. Schrock had filed a Freedom of Information Request for all documents pertaining to the disappearance and "presumed murder" of her husband, Nicholas Wickman Schrock. The author filed his request in 1989.

In a cable dated January 20, 1987, the Consulate in Mazatlán reported that they had contacted the Mazatlán office of the federal attorney general for advice on how best to pursue the investigation. The Mexican officials in Mazatlán replied that the files had been forwarded to their office in Mexico City. Mazatlán's cable also noted that the Consulate's October 22, 1986, letter to the state attorney general remained unanswered.

On Thursday, April 9 the Principal Officer at the Consulate in Mazatlán wrote a long letter to the new Sinaloa Attorney General Manuel Lazcano Ochoa in which he noted, among other things. that it had been two years since the remains of Professor Schrock were recovered. In that time little progress had been made. The letter asked specific questions and urged the state of Sinaloa to renew the investigation into the death of Professor Schrock. There is no indication in the files that this letter was ever answered.

On April 13 the Consulate reported that it had again raised the issue of the investigation with the federal attorney general's office in Mazatlán to no avail. The Embassy in Mexico City wrote to the Mexican foreign ministry on Tuesday, June 9 requesting a status report on the Schrock case. The final substantive message in the files sent to me by the Department of State is a cable dated January 19, 1988. Most of the cable refers to other matters, but the one relevant passage regarding the investigation regarding Professor Nicholas Wickham Schrock is the simple statement:

"No activity has been apparent in case."

AFTERWORD

We will probably never know what happened to Professor Schrock on that lonely stretch of highway in Mexico during the summer of 1982. There are many plausible theories. He might have been killed by "El Pájaro" and "El Nene" after stopping at the filling station in Coyotitán, but the evidence does not seem to support this theory. He could have been similarly killed by the police from San Ignacio. That is quite plausible, but I doubt it. My view is that the policemen were just opportunists who found the vehicle and appropriated it for their own use after pilfering the contents. They certainly paid for their decisions, as they must have thought that their law enforcement status allowed them to act with impunity.

It is also questionable whether Professor Schrock ever stopped at the filling station in Coyotitán. While many of the later cables note this was the last place he was seen alive, the only evidence I have seen regarding this issue was made in recanted confessions that were allegedly made under duress. Another theory that was put forth in several different forms was that Professor Schrock was killed in a case of mistaken identity by members of drug cartels, or possibly on the orders of "Cochiloco." Again, I personally strongly doubt this scenario, but after forty years it looks like we will never know.

There were reports around the time of the Professor's

disappearance of Mexican citizens being robbed along the stretch of highway between Culiacán and Mazatlán by persons falsely claiming to be policemen. It is at least plausible that Professor Schrock ran afoul of these individuals and that something went wrong. The fact that the body was buried near where the truck was abandoned and the fact they left the truck points to the possibility that it was a botched robbery. The murderers might also have just waited at the detour around the bridgework. I drove that detour shortly after the Professor disappeared and it was both isolated and very rough, so a vehicle would have had to drive very slowly over that portion and could have easily been stopped and the driver robbed. A plausible scenario, but again it is nothing more than that. Whatever the case, Professor Schrock was just a good man driving through Mexico for an enjoyable summer of teaching and exploring who somehow fate led in a different direction.

I have wanted to write this story for the last forty years. It had a profound influence on my life and my career. It gave me a stronger commitment to the State Department and public service. I also wanted to show a broader audience a series of events from the viewpoint of Foreign Service Officers serving abroad and trying to protect American citizens. The events during the search for Professor Schrock also had an important influence on other consular officers and State Department employees. Throughout my 35-year career as a Foreign Service Officer, colleagues, on hearing my name, would ask if I was the officer that was involved in the Nicholas Schrock case. Several decades after the events in Mexico while I was attending the State Department's retirement course, an officer that I didn't know approached me and asked if I was the Robert Downes that had served in Mexico in the early 1980s. After admitting I was, he said he had been one of a group of junior Foreign Service Officers working in the visa section in Guadalajara. He said that each night the group would get together and read the latest cable that I, or others in Mazatlán or Hermosillo, had written about the case. He said the same was true of another large group of vice consuls stationed in Monterrey and Mexico City who followed the case closely. He said it gave them real insight into the State Department's consular work abroad and into operations of the various levels of Mexican criminal enforcement agencies. It also gave them added confidence in their commitment to the Foreign Service as a career.

A final note. Some years after the body of Professor Schrock was finally identified, shipped to the United States, and laid to rest, I was approached by another of the vice consuls who had worked on the search for Professor Schrock after I left Mexico. He said one thing always bothered him about the case. He read in my notes and inventory that the San Ignacio police had found a watch in Professor Schrock's truck which was used in evidence by the prosecution against them and eventually returned to Mrs. Schrock. I verified his understanding of the facts. "Why then," he asked, "was the body that was eventually found in 1985 and identified as Professor Schrock wearing a watch? Who travels with two watches?" It had clearly troubled him for some years and I could understand why. It implied the body was somehow not that of the Professor. In this case I could at least reassure him. Mrs. Schrock had told me her husband liked to time things and so had a new (for then) digital watch for timing, but also carried a dress watch. Both watches matched the description of the watches he was traveling with according to what Mrs. Schrock had told me forty years ago.

ACKNOWLEDGEMENTS

I could not have written this book without the assistance of my daughter Laura, who has helped my writing dream come true. My wife Sara provided consistent support and invaluable technical knowledge on writing in the genre of true crime. My good friend -- and frequent fellow explorer in Mexico and Guatemala -- retired journalist Michael Cárdenaz was generous in his time in reviewing and editing my draft. I must also note the contribution of my good friends Michael Oreste and Russell Frisbie who served in Mazatlán as vice consuls and worked on the search for Professor Schrock. They were generous in providing their time to let me pick their memories regarding the case. Many of the participants, such as John St. Denis, Elayne Urban and Ambassador John Gavin are no longer with us, but they contributed in their own way. While I tried to contact former Vice Consul Douglas R. Smith, I was unable to find him. Given his tireless efforts to search for Professor Schrock, I am sure this book would have benefited from his sharp intellect and insightful observations. Finally, I have to acknowledge the excellent and comprehensive work of the State Department's Freedom of Information Act staff, who provided me with literally hundreds of pages of relevant information used in supplementing my memory in writing this book. The State Department's clearance office was also efficient and helpful in reviewing this book for publication.

ABOUT THE AUTHOR

Robert Richard Downes

Robert Richard Downes is a retired Senior Foreign Service Officer with 37 years of federal service, the majority served overseas with the U.S. State Department. During his first tour with the State Department, he investigated the disappearance of Professor Schrock. Downes worked in Australia, Germany, Guatemala, Mexico, Nicaragua, Thailand, and Venezuela. He now lives in his native Texas where he actively kayaks, writes, and volunteers for local charities and international organizations.

Made in the USA
Columbia, SC
06 June 2023